GUERRILLA
MUM

of related interest

Choosing a School for a Child With Special Needs
Ruth Birnbaum
ISBN 978 1 84310 987 7

Supportive Parenting
Becoming an Advocate for your Child with Special Needs
Jan Starr Campito
ISBN 978 1 84310 851 1

Successful School Change and Transition for the Child with Asperger Syndrome
A Guide for Parents
Clare Lawrence
ISBN 978 1 84905 052 4

How to Make School Make Sense
A Parents' Guide to Helping the Child with Asperger Syndrome
Clare Lawrence
Foreword by Tony Attwood
ISBN 978 1 84310 664 7

GUERRILLA
MUM

Surviving the Special Educational Needs Jungle

ELLEN POWER

Jessica Kingsley *Publishers*
London and Philadelphia

First published in 2010
by Jessica Kingsley Publishers
116 Pentonville Road
London N1 9JB, UK
and
400 Market Street, Suite 400
Philadelphia, PA 19106, USA

www.jkp.com

Peterborough City Council	
60000 0000 56061	
Askews & Holts	Feb-2012
371.904	£14.99

Library of Congress Cataloging in Publication Data
A CIP catalog record for this book is available from the Library of Congress

British Library Cataloguing in Publication Data
A CIP catalogue record for this book is available from the British Library

ISBN 978 1 84310 999 0

Printed and bound in Great Britain by
MPG Books Group

For my husband and my children, Peter and William.
Also for JY and AJ, without whom we
would have achieved nothing.

ACKNOWLEDGEMENTS

Thank you to my family for supporting me in the writing of this book and for understanding why it was so important to me to do it. Thank you also to the teachers, teaching assistants, health professionals and others who have helped us to meet the needs of our children. Thank you to the staff at JKP.

CONTENTS

LIST OF ABBREVIATIONS

CDC Child Development Centre

DCSF Department for Children, Schools and Families

DED Disability Equality Duty

EHRC Equality and Human Rights Commission

HESC Health, Education and Social Care

IEP Individual Education Plan

IPSEA Independent Panel for Special Educational Advice

KS1/KS2 Key Stage 1/Key Stage 2

LEA Local Education Authority (at present these are known simply as Local Authorities, or LAs)

PTA Parent–Teacher Association

SEN Special Educational Needs

SENDIST Special Educational Needs and Disability Tribunal (now First-tier Tribunal (Special Educational Needs and Disability))

SENCO Special Educational Needs Co-ordinator

SENR Special Educational Needs Register

SNO Special Needs Officer

TA Teaching Assistant

PREFACE

This is the true story of a guerrilla mum. I know it sounds strange, but then so is my story. It tells how I changed from being a mild mannered mother of two beautiful boys, to an experienced fighter against officialdom in local government and the NHS. Seven years ago I believed in our health and education services' ability to meet the needs of my disabled children. I believed that if they ever needed medical help, or help for special educational needs, then they would get it because they were entitled to it. I have gone through a process of sadness, disillusionment and sorrow, as my children's needs were trivialised, ignored or, at times, completely denied. Faced with the option of failing my children or going to the private system, I decided to fight back. On this road many battles have been won and my children now have appropriate education and healthcare provision. However, the war continues to be fought.

Anybody with children in the state education system should be able to access the services we have obtained for our boys. We pay for them in our taxes and national insurance contributions. We should not have to pay again through paying for private assessment, therapies or schools. It is undeniable that some parents are able to meet their children's needs by paying for expensive schools, doctors and therapists but like many parents, we simply could not afford to spend money on these things. Nevertheless, we have succeeded in meeting our children's needs by the use of services available through local education authorities, the state school system and the NHS.

Our priority is to meet our children's needs. Local education authorities and NHS Trusts have other priorities, government targets and financial restrictions. In my view they use every trick in the book to reduce their outgoings and meet their own financial targets at the expense of our children. They get away with this because parents accept the view of the 'expert', don't challenge, and don't cause a fuss.

If they object they hold back because they do not want their child to be penalised as a result. This book is based on how we learned lessons and achieved results by challenging, making a fuss and pushing the relevant authorities to meet their obligations. Of course all these things have a cost and we have suffered en route to success through our own naivety and by not knowing the hidden rules by which the system works.

If you want to obtain the right services for your child, read on and benefit from our experiences.

Note: For ease of understanding both boys and girls are referred to using the pronouns 'he' and 'him'.

THE LAW COVERED
IN THIS BOOK

The law in the UK is complex and multi-layered, with England and Wales, Northern Ireland and Scotland operating separate systems. Put simply, England and Wales follow one legal system, but since the establishment of the Welsh Assembly Wales now has limited powers to legislate for itself and there may be some differences between English and Welsh law and policy. The law in Northern Ireland and Scotland is quite different again and a lot of it is administered locally. Please see the Useful Organisations and Web Resources section for contact details for the different administrative centres for England and Wales, Northern Ireland and Scotland. The specific law that I refer to in the book applies to England and Wales, as this has been my point of reference when meeting my own children's needs. For Northern Ireland and Scotland please find information about the law by contacting the relevant organisations in my resources section. Please bear in mind that although I have done all I can to ensure the accuracy of what I have written about the law I am not a lawyer. My aim is not to teach the law but to show how parents can develop a good enough understanding of the law to challenge those in authority and meet their children's special educational needs. As the law is an organic and constantly changing entity, readers should check with the relevant information and parent support organisations that any legislation, policy or guidelines mentioned in this book haven't been changed after the time of writing.

Chapter 1

IDENTIFYING
SPECIAL NEEDS

All parents hope to be able to do their best for their children. However, this goal becomes more difficult to achieve when your child has special educational needs. Suddenly, getting the right education for your child is more about meeting their specific learning needs, rather than simply catchment areas, league tables and the usual concerns that parents have. It can be extremely difficult to meet an individual's specific learning needs without accessing additional funding in our education system. It seems to subscribe very much to a 'one size fits all' philosophy, and although there is room for a limited amount of variation, children in state schools generally all get the same education. If your child can cope with the limited amount of help in the mainstream classroom that can be provided to children who do not have statements, then they will most probably be fine. However, if they need extra help in terms of teaching assistant (TA) support, specialist equipment and/or teaching, specialist therapies, an individually modified curriculum and extra time for exams, for example, then your children will have difficulty in fulfilling their potential at school.

Current figures show that around one in a hundred children have some form of autism. It is estimated that around 10 per cent of children have dyspraxia and that this figure is climbing. Government statistics bear out the fact that one in five of all children will at some point in their time at school have special educational needs.

Both of our children have special educational needs. Our oldest son Peter is currently aged 13. He has Asperger Syndrome, along with dyspraxia, ADHD, OCD, handwriting difficulties, and some orthopaedic problems. Our younger child, William, is now aged 11 and has been diagnosed with motor dyspraxia and severe verbal dyspraxia. He also has handwriting difficulties. As our children moved through their nursery and KS1 education, we watched with growing dismay as they failed and fell further and further behind their peers both educationally and socially. Repeated visits to school to discuss their progress – or the lack of it – led us nowhere. Whatever the school offered to do, it always seemed to be too little, too late and hopelessly inadequate in meeting their needs. It took us several years to work out that our children actually had significant special educational needs, and that there was already a system in place for meeting those needs – the statementing process. Further discussion with our children's school left us utterly confused when it appeared that our children were not eligible to benefit from this system. We were told that they 'weren't bad enough for a statement', they were 'too clever', and that the statementing system was not for children with 'speech problems'. We were told that they couldn't have a statement because they were not 'in the bottom 2 per cent of the population in terms of academic achievement'. From what our children's teachers told us, even if the school tried to get our children a statement, 'it would be no good! They didn't statement children like Peter and William.' Statementing was only for the children with the most severe difficulties. None of the above is true, and as we slowly found this out, we began to trust our children's teachers less and less. What did all this mean? Were our children not failing? They were, and the gap between them and their peers was widening, rather than closing. Were they not in need of more help than the school appeared to be able to offer them? Most definitely! It was all very puzzling as those very people (teachers, doctors, local education authority officials) who should have been helping our children to achieve at school, dug in their heels and did all they could to put us off getting statements for both of our children. We quite literally did not know where to turn.

Several years on, and following a struggle that was traumatic and difficult for both us and out children, Peter and William now have statements of special educational need. A statement is a legally binding document, enshrined in the law that identifies our children's special educational needs in school and documents the funding, provision and resources needed to meet those needs. The local education authority and our children's schools are obliged by the law to do what the statement tells them to do to help our children, and there are legal consequences if they do not comply with it. Our children's rights to have help at school are protected by their statements. Without these, William and Peter would not be able to access the curriculum or make progress at school. We know this because since they have had their statements, we have been able to watch them succeed, and now they are thriving. We know that these documents have been vital to them in accessing the curriculum and in making the progress we always knew them to be capable of.

The schools of today have a difficult time in coping with the volume of children needing extra support in the classroom. This is in part due to increasing awareness among some parents about special educational needs and these parents are already asking that their children receive extra help at school. It is also due to the fact that mainstream schools are placed under increased pressure to meet the needs of a wider range of children. This is because in recent years the government has aimed to increase inclusion in mainstream schools and to reduce the number of children being placed in special schools. Many special schools have been closed, and a lot of the children who might have been placed in special schools a few years ago are now in mainstream schools.

The great majority of children who have special educational needs do not have a statement. This means that they do not have access to the extra funding a statement might bring. Their needs must be met from within their school's already stretched resources, as it tries to use any special needs funding to help as many children as possible. These children can easily lose any support they may have if their school decides it can no longer afford it. Children who have statements benefit from having an amount of funding and services specifically designed to meet their own individual needs, and this cannot be taken away due to a lack of financial resources. However, complex new funding arrangements for schools (which I will go into later) mean that, from the point of view of the head teacher, it is not always financially beneficial to the wider school to have children in the school with statements, as sometimes the schools themselves now have to fund statements from their own special needs budgets. I can really understand that head teachers in schools have difficult decisions to make. They have to make the funding that is available work for all children in their school and are focused on 'the many', whereas parents are naturally concerned mainly with their own children. This is why parents must play a pivotal role in having their children's special educational needs identified, assessed and met: sometimes, they are the only ones who have the time, dedication and knowledge of the child that is required to get a statement in place.

So where do we, as parents begin? How do we decide whether any special needs that our children might have are being met at school? The acid test really is, whether our children are making progress at school. Even little children at school are tested in some way by their teachers, and even in KS1 your child's teacher will know how they are doing in comparison with their peers. Ask! All parents should satisfy themselves that they know how their child is doing at school. If they have special needs, then they themselves must find out all they can about it and understand their child's level of need. If their child's needs are designated by the school as 'mild', parents should make certain that this is the case, that their needs are being met in school and that the child in question is making proper progress. If this does not happen over a reasonable period of time, regardless of what any teacher might say, then this is the time that we should start to be seriously concerned about whether our child's needs are being met.

If any of the issues raised so far is familiar to you, read on.

Guerrilla Tip

🐾 Remember, only children with a statement of special educational needs have their rights to support in school protected by law.

This is a good point to introduce the *Guerrilla Mum Mantra: Don't take no for an answer, never give up. If in doubt, telephone, email and write letters.*

All the other advice I give is absolutely reliant on the mantra being followed. We knew for years before our children were diagnosed that they had significant difficulties. Many professionals we approached were of the opinion that our children were just quirky, were 'fine', they may well 'grow out of it', or that we should wait and see what happened when they were older, thereby losing valuable time to help them. Early intervention is the key to children overcoming developmental difficulties.

FIRST SIGNS THAT YOUR CHILD MAY HAVE SPECIAL EDUCATIONAL NEEDS

Enough time has now elapsed for us to be able to look back on all the indicators that our children had difficulties. Some examples of these indicators are below. Some things may ring a bell with other parents but frankly, if you are worried about anything at all, follow it up. Obviously I am not a child development expert, but these are the issues around our own children's development that made us stop and think there may be a problem.

Is your child meeting his motor milestones?

It really does matter if your child attains the motor milestones on the development charts within the time limits set. In many other areas, it is perfectly OK for a child to be an individual but child development is not one of these areas. Although there is room for some variation in the standards set, generally speaking, if a child is unusually slow to lift his head, to learn to sit up or to crawl, or walk, these things are a real indicator of possible difficulties, which should have the child's doctor sitting up and taking notice.

Is your child slow to speak?

Does your child struggle to speak or to make any noises at all? Does your child seem to be very much behind other children their age in these terms? If this is so it is important to get an early referral to a speech therapist to identify why.

Does your child have difficulty understanding language?

Does your child hear what people say, but not respond appropriately? Does your child have problems understanding what is said to him? If so this could be an indicator of a language delay and needs to be checked out by a speech and language therapist.

Does your child have difficulties socially?

Does your child understand how to play with other children? Does he try to change the rules to suit himself, oblivious to what anyone else might think of that? Does your child interact appropriately with other children? If social interaction problems persist it is a good idea to have your child assessed by a paediatrician to find out why this may be.

Does your child limit which foods he will eat, even if quite hungry?

Many children are picky eaters. However, some children with developmental disorders take this to a whole new level! Children with special needs may be bothered by food textures and might self-limit the food they are prepared to put into their mouths, even if they happen to be quite hungry. If this situation persists despite your best efforts to introduce a varied diet to your child it should be addressed by a paediatrician, especially if a child's weight gain is compromised.

Can your child follow only one instruction at once?

Children with language or processing issues often find it difficult to follow more than one instruction at once. An example of this is 'Go to the front door, pick up your shoes and come back to me with them.' If your child is still at the front door five minutes later (or never got there!) and if this sort of thing happens regularly, you may have a problem.

Can your child pretend?

A lack of imagination is one of the impairments experienced by children on the autistic spectrum. If your child does not pretend and has very 'concrete' play, this can, along with other indicators show that an assessment by a paediatrician is needed to either rule in or out the condition.

Does your child avoid colouring in, or seem to be unable to put pen to paper?

Children with a range of developmental conditions including dyspraxia, ADHD, autism, or motor problems frequently display immature pencil skills or art work. Often they refuse to pick up a pencil or crayon at all. This has many implications for school because if they do not develop pencil skills they will be unable to record their own school work.

Does your child have obsessions or enthusiasms?

Many children on the autistic spectrum become obsessed with a specialist subject and can become very distressed if they cannot pursue it. It could be a love of *Star Wars*, Thomas the Tank Engine, car number plates, gardening, books, Harry Potter, or simply anything round. It can be literally anything.

Lots of children not on the autistic spectrum have enthusiasms but the key point here is whether or not your child can be persuaded to put it to one side willingly and to come and do something else.

Does your child need a fixed routine?

How does your child react if his routine is changed suddenly? Does change lead to tantrums? Children on the autistic spectrum, can become very distressed when the routine they expect to happen is suddenly changed without warning.

Is your child an angel at school and a devil at home?

If a child has special needs the stress of being in school and trying to keep up with everything, especially if they are motivated to succeed, can be extremely stressful. They may be extremely well behaved at school but let off steam at home with explosive or aggressive behaviour.

Trust your instincts

Many parents just *know* that there is something different about their child. There is nothing specific that they can identify in words, but when their child is later diagnosed with a difficulty, they are not surprised because there always was something they 'could not put their finger on' about their child. If you are one of these parents, or if you see similar things to those listed above in your child or children and want to get them some help, there are a number of things you can do to help them.

ACCESSING EARLY INTERVENTION SERVICES

Once we felt reasonably confident that our children had special needs we wanted to do something tangible to help them. We did not know it at the time but this was the point at which we began to be our children's *advocates*. I found it enormously helpful for me to separate this role from being my children's mother. The word 'advocate' can be defined as someone who campaigns for a particular cause, or a person who acts on someone else's behalf. If you decide that the time has come to get help at school for your child, you will find yourself doing both of these things and more. This role requires that you develop new skills alongside your parenting skills so that you can negotiate with the school, local education authority and health authority for the help your child will need to be able to be successful at school. It will also be necessary to establish what level of help your child will need, and if he will need a statement in order to be able to access the National Curriculum. You don't have to know everything straight away, just who to ask.

How does one reach the decision to pursue further help at school for a child, or indeed, a statement? It is a big decision to make, the child may acquire a label which no parent wants and many parents fear will stick to their child forever. You won't want to feel that your child's teachers will lower their expectations of him because of a label. For us, it was an easy decision to pursue a diagnosis and indeed a statement for both of our children. Without a diagnosis, or a label, we saw many years ahead for them where they would struggle through school with their needs unidentified and unmet. Any concern about them losing opportunities in life because of a label paled into insignificance when we realised that if their needs were not identified quickly, this would also lead to a loss of opportunity – quite possibly a much bigger loss. This is an important decision that each parent must reach for themselves based on what is known about their child. We decided at that point to actively pursue a diagnosis and to try to get a diagnosis for both of our children. This meant attending lots of appointments.

Guerrilla Tips

- Once your child begins to access medical, educational or therapeutic services begin to take notes at all meetings.
- Store your notes in a box or filing cabinet in a place where it is easy to find information.
- If professionals send you reports about your child store these in the same place.
- Some people find the easiest storage method is to keep all correspondence about a particular child together, in date order, as it arrives, to provide a 'snapshot' of their child at any one time.
- If you have meetings to discuss your child's needs, make a record of the meeting and send it to those involved by email or post. If nobody disputes your meeting minutes this can be taken as tacit agreement that they are accurate.

Remember the *Guerrilla Mum Mantra: Don't take no for an answer, never give up. If in doubt, telephone, email and write letters.*

Below are listed some of the services you may need to use if it is suspected that your child may have special educational needs, and you wish to access treatment or therapies or to build up a picture of their difficulties and needs.

Health visitor

Sometimes special needs are identified by professionals who will spot something that concerns them in a child. This is quite likely to be your health visitor who will commence routine appointments with you and your child once your midwife bows out of the picture a couple of weeks after your child is born. In the early days these key people are an excellent port of call if you do become concerned about your child's development or health. Not only that, they know what they are looking for in children who are developing normally, and will spot things that remain invisible to the rose coloured spectacles of the new parent. I was that parent! Make friends with your health visitor and establish a good rapport. If you need them, they will see you in your home often, and will get to know your child very well in its natural environment. The health visitor will be happy to answer questions or find out answers for you so don't be afraid of asking about any concerns you may have yourself. For us, our health visitor was the first independent person who said she thought that something was wrong with our children. In both of our children's cases, developmental milestones were missed. Some milestones were quite subtle and we needed to hear the health visitor's perspective. With Peter, we already knew that he had some physical disabilities and we sort of suspected that there might be other problems but when you are with your beautiful son 24 hours a day you don't think about these things. An objective view helps everyone. If your health visitor does pick out problems, you are likely to be very shocked and having a supportive professional involved can help you through the stages you will go through in accepting your child's difficulty. However, it is very important that you understand it is your responsibility to become very active in getting help for your child from the health and education services.

One of our mistakes was that we assumed the system would 'kick in' following identification of difficulties in Peter. We naively waited for therapists to knock on our door, expecting that they would form an orderly queue to help us. The truth is that the system is there, but the emphasis is very much on the parent to get involved in meeting their child's needs. It is very easy for children to slip through the net because if you don't make approaches to the relevant professionals, they won't know about your child and it is very likely that nothing will happen. Parents can minimise the chance of this happening if they enquire about services for their child, make appointments, and basically go about 'rattling the cages' of anyone they can think of whom they think may be able to help their child. Health visitors can help you by referring you directly to services which they think are relevant to your child or by speaking to your GP. They are also useful as recorders of evidence, as they do keep records on children. Take them to appointments with you if you think you need them (although they might not always be able to come with you), and make sure they are on the circulation list, by name, of any reports that are written about your child. You should take notes too! Our health visitor was wonderful. She was the first to notice Peter's difficulties and pointed us in the right direction. She remains a friend.

Medical services and therapists

When your child is referred to medical services and therapists it is important to make certain that you ask all the questions you have and to make a note of the responses. When you have appointments with your GP, remember that not all GPs are sensitive to child development matters. Ask friends and other parents if they know which GP at the practice is the best with children. Then go and see this person and ask their opinion. Almost certainly, this will lead to you asking for a referral to see a specialist or to the local Child Development Centre. Continuing to keep accurate records will ensure that you will have the ammunition you require to carry on the battle for your son or daughter.

When you go to the LEA and ask them to assess your child, your medical information will form a large part of the evidence you submit in support of your request. Evidence is essential. With evidence help can still be denied, but without evidence, you have no hope at all of getting what your child needs. The earlier you can get your child some help the better his chances are of overcoming his difficulties.

Guerrilla Tips

- Make good use of all the child health services on offer to you as a young family. They often spot problems early and put parents in a position to do something about them.

- It is vital that you think about what can be done rather than what the health service or education services can afford to do.

- Don't accept second best.

- Don't be afraid if you think your child may be labelled as a result of accessing help through medical services. Sometimes this is the only way to get help, and a label can quite literally open doors that would otherwise remain shut.

- If you happen to work for health or education services try to separate this from being your child's advocate. Forget about budgets, targets and how strapped for cash your colleagues say they are. You do not have to apologise for trying to secure the best services for your child.

- Your notes and records will form the evidence you need if your child later needs a statement. Keep them in good order so you can find information as you need it.

- Fight for your child – you cannot rely on anyone else to do it for you!

Your child's difficulties may well not be clear in the early days and you may need to obtain referrals to a number of medical services to unravel what those needs are. More often than not, a diagnosis has been the key to our children being able to obtain services. A diagnosis has also helped inform the content of our children's statements, to enable teachers to understand their difficulties and how to teach them.

So does a child need a medical diagnosis to get a statement? Surely if a statement is all about special educational needs, you shouldn't actually need a medical diagnosis to have these needs met? Unfortunately, the system seems to favour those with a diagnosis. Special educational needs (SEN) are diagnosed formally through tests administered by doctors and therapists and teachers, and having a medical label certainly seems (in my experience) to help a lot with getting a statement. Children will also need a label or diagnosis to access specialist provision such as a place in a speech and language unit, hearing support unit, Asperger's unit, a placement in a special school and so on. William needed a diagnosis of severe verbal dyspraxia to meet the criteria for a place in a specialist speech and language unit. Without this he would quite simply have not been eligible for the six years of specialist speech therapy he needed. Peter needed a diagnosis of Asperger Syndrome to get the help and support he now has in his statement to enable him to access the curriculum at school.

Parents facing the prospect that their children might have special needs can often feel overwhelmed. We certainly did! The good news is that parents do not have to figure out their child's problems alone. Children can be assessed by paediatricians and a range of therapists through your local hospital. These people will be specially trained to work with children. In our area we can access the community paediatricians' service through the Child Development Centre.

The Child Development Centre

The purpose of the CDC is to monitor and manage the care and treatment of children with illnesses and developmental difficulties. In our area the CDC is associated with a community-based team and it is these doctors, rather than the GP, who are approached for relevant medical reports when statutory assessments are being made by the local education authority. If you think your child needs a statement it will help if your child is already known to a paediatrician. Peter's initial referral to this service was made by our GP as a result of our health visitor's concerns following several months' observation. He was one year old. Once a paediatrician has assessed a child at the CDC, they may then refer children on to other clinics within the hospital, and can monitor progress.

At our first appointment at the CDC the assessment process began with the most obvious thing – Peter's orthopaedic and movement problems. Following this assessment he was referred by the paediatrician to a physiotherapist to try and get him through the physical development milestones he had missed. This was our introduction to the round of hospital appointments that still forms part of our lives.

Eyesight testing and hearing tests

As you probably already know, all children receive free hearing and eyesight tests. Each child is tested at various intervals before they start school. The idea is to pick up any difficulties that your child may have early, so that they may receive all the help they need at school if they turn out to have a problem with either their hearing or their eyesight. Just because a child might 'pass' these tests at one point does not mean that their status cannot change. If you suspect any difficulty with hearing or eyesight, have these tests carried out again.

Guerrilla Tips

- 🐾 A referral to a paediatrician can open the doors to referrals to a range of relevant services for your child.
- 🐾 If your child has reading difficulties at school double check that he does not have a vision problem, even if he has previously passed eye tests!
- 🐾 Always attend hearing checks – hearing problems are easy to miss but make a big difference to behaviour and ability to learn.

Other types of intervention

There are various types of therapies available on the NHS to help your child overcome developmental difficulties and to develop his skills. Below some of the services you may encounter when your child is referred to the CDC are described in more detail. Children who are missing their milestones may be referred to services such as physiotherapy, speech therapy and occupational therapy through their health visitor or their GP to try and help them meet these milestones. This is not an exhaustive list of the health services available but it is a starting point. Both of our children use or have used these services. The working relationship can be a long one, and it is vital to build positive relationships with therapists and practitioners. Here is some information about who they are and what they can do for your child.

PHYSIOTHERAPY

The paediatric physiotherapist will assess, treat and manage children who have a range of disabilities, illnesses, movement disorders or muscular or skeletal problems or orthopaedic problems. Referral is most likely to be via a paediatrician, consultant, other doctor or health professional. If the child has started school, then the school may make the referral. Physiotherapists work within the context of the child's family and school so that both parents and teachers can be involved in any therapy that is recommended. They also form part of a multidisciplinary approach to helping children and frequently work with other therapists and medical services with the aim of helping the child. Following assessment a treatment plan is produced, with the participation of parents, carers, and school staff. The treatment plan will include an action plan in which goals are set and the child is regularly assessed to check if the goals have been reached. The family and school are important figures in the success of a child accessing physiotherapy services, as they are the key people who will work with the child on a daily basis.

The paediatric physiotherapist will develop a plan to move your child through any missed physical developmental milestones by using a range of exercises and therapy through play. He can also enable your child to access therapeutic toys to use in therapy. Peter didn't learn to walk until he was 22 months old and he used a special push-along trolley to develop his walking skills. Trolleys available through general toy shops did not suit him as he used to trip over them, but a specialised trolley from the CDC toy library was a real help to him gaining his mobility. I am convinced that without this particular trolley Peter would have walked much later than he did.

Physiotherapists use observation and standardised tests to diagnose a range of conditions. Our children were diagnosed with dyspraxia following the use of the Miller Joint Assessment test in which their skills were assessed and scored. These tests eventually led to diagnoses of dyspraxia being made. These have been critical in obtaining services for them at their school. Of course, there are a range of other tests for other difficulties that your physiotherapist can use as appropriate to help with diagnosis and a physiotherapist can discuss these with parents.

Guerrilla Tips

🐾 If a physiotherapist gives you exercises to do with your child, *do them*. Failure to do the exercises will hinder your child's progress and your child's therapist will be able to tell!

🐾 If your child's condition is likely to impact on their PE curriculum at school, their physiotherapist will be the key to the school's ability to devise a safe and enjoyable individualised PE curriculum. It is the responsibility of the Special Educational Needs Co-ordinator (SENCO) to arrange for this to happen.

🐾 Make certain that any reports the physiotherapist may write are also sent to your child's school. The SENCO may pick up on this and arrange with the physiotherapist to visit your child and his teachers in school. If this does not happen, you will need to request that such a meeting is arranged.

Remember the Guerrilla Mum Mantra: Don't take no for an answer, never give up. If in doubt, telephone, email and write letters.

SPEECH AND LANGUAGE THERAPY

If your child does not achieve the developmental milestones relating to speech and language, your health visitor, GP or paediatrician will make a referral to a paediatric speech and language therapist. Such a referral can also be made by your child's school. It is the speech therapist's aim to enable each child to communicate effectively and also to ensure that the child is able to develop good eating and drinking skills.

The speech therapist works very methodically and uses standardised tests to identify and diagnose difficulties. Whereas other therapy services may wait a while to get to know children, or may use therapy time to concentrate on a range of games to promote motor development, in my experience speech therapists tend to get out the standardised tests very quickly in order to establish a base line – to find out what the child's strengths and weaknesses are, and to find out why they are having difficulty with communication. It is really important to understand what type of communication difficulty a child has. This is because there are lots of different types of speech difficulties and they all need different therapy. It is crucial to match each kind of difficulty with the correct type of therapy. For example, children with language problems have difficulty understanding language to an age-appropriate level. This can lead to problems with social interaction and with learning. They also have problems making their wants and needs understood. They need therapy that stimulates their language development. Children with speech articulation problems on the other hand understand language to an age-appropriate level, and they also know what they would like to say. They just cannot correctly articulate their speech and as a result people do not understand them. Putting them into a group therapy session with children working on language development skills will do them absolutely no good at all, and will lead to frustration and no progress will be seen. If speech and language needs are not addressed this can in the short term lead to frustration and in the long term leaves children with low self-esteem, social interaction difficulties and low educational attainment. It is very important that children with speech and language problems are appropriately assessed so that they can receive the right kind of therapy.

Guerrilla Tips

- Early intervention is the key to recovery from speech and language disorder, so get help as early as possible.
- Once your child is referred to a speech and language therapist, bear in mind that it is essential that speech and language problems are diagnosed accurately to ensure that the right type of therapy is prescribed.
- If your child receives a therapy that after a reasonable amount of time does not seem to be working or 'right', do not be afraid to discuss this with the service provider with the aim of improving the service your child can receive. Get help with this from the Patient Advice and Liaison Service if you need it. Contact details are in the Useful Organisations and Web Resources section.

Make certain that the school receives a copy of the speech therapy reports. Your child's speech and language therapist should work in partnership with you and your child's school in achieving your child's speech and language therapy objectives.

OCCUPATIONAL THERAPY

Your child may be referred to an occupational therapist (OT), if he develops difficulties with learning the practical skills required for daily life. The aim of the OT will be to enable your child to develop the practical and social skills necessary for him to become as independent as possible. A child may be referred to the OT by his health visitor, nursery, doctor or school. In some areas, parents can refer their own child to the OT service but it will be necessary to check if local referral criteria allow this. Once the referral is made, the child's case will be looked at to check the referral is appropriate and to establish a reasonable timescale for seeing the child. When you attend your first appointment the therapist will find out from you why you are concerned about your child and will assess him to find out in which skill areas he needs help. The appointment may take place at your home, school, or within hospital clinics, or a mixture of venues. When helping your child with skills he is likely to use at school, it makes sense to visit the child there with his teachers. Assessment will include dressing, eating and toileting skills. It will cover school skills such as using scissors or pencil control. OTs can also help with sensory issues, play skills and movement or gross motor skills. For older children they can look at developing independence or life skills.

You will always receive a report outlining the findings of any assessment. A report will also be sent to your child's school and the referrer if that wasn't you. It will outline your child's difficulties and make recommendations as to how he may be supported in his family environment, and at school. It may also generate a new referral to other services, for example, a physiotherapist, if gross motor difficulties are established. Support may mean giving training to parents or teachers. OTs may decide to work with your child in school, and your child may have individual therapy or group therapy. It is important that your child's fine motor difficulties are correctly diagnosed. Peter has always had handwriting problems and still could not hold a pencil properly at the age of 12. He was nine before an OT examined his hands to find very loose ligaments in his fingers and explained why it was so painful for him to try and write. This also enabled school to see that handwriting programmes were pointless and that other more suitable means of recording his work should be found.

Guerrilla Tips

You have a right to attend:

- 🐾 appointments your child may have with a professional in school
- 🐾 assessments of your child by any professional in school.

You may choose to wait outside and talk to the therapist or professional afterwards if you think your presence may adversely affect your child's performance or behaviour during the appointment or assessment.

PURSUING A DIAGNOSIS

It may well be that your child has mild difficulties. So long as there is a steady supply of information from their paediatrician or therapists, and the school acts on this information to devise an effective individualised teaching programme, all will be well. Involvement with these services may lead to a diagnosis – or it may be that no diagnosis is forthcoming. It also needs to be said that if your child does not have an official diagnosis, and a school is so minded, it can more easily categorise difficulties as being 'mild' or 'minimal', and your child may never get the right level of help. It was only when we realised that without a diagnosis, the school would be happy to continue offering Peter and William minimal amounts of help that we began to think about pursuing a diagnosis for each of them.

Sometimes a diagnosis is very clear and doctors do not hesitate to make that diagnosis. At other times it is less clear cut and a child could quite easily go through life undiagnosed. Many children are only diagnosed when their parents insist on pursuing this route.

It is very difficult to decide how a child may benefit from a diagnosis. It can be quite scary to contemplate a label that must be carried for life. I had a number of years in which to come to terms with my own children's very apparent difficulties and felt very positive about their receiving a diagnosis. However, I know that many parents will struggle with the news and this deserves some thought. Nobody really expects that they will one day have a child with special needs. We all have expectations about the children that we might one day have, and rarely does a disabled child form a part of that dream. It is therefore a tremendous shock when parents find out that their lives are about to change in this way and that they will have to change their life plans to meet the needs of such a child. It is truly strong parents who can view this news positively, and assert to themselves and the world that they fully accept and celebrate their disabled child. Few of us are like this. Families mostly go through some process of sadness, anger and grief, and parents are the hardest hit by this news. Some people never come to accept this and remain stuck in sadness, anger or grief. However you deal with the news, there are some things that remain the same for all of us. Your child is going to need you to fight his corner at school and in life, much more than if he were a child born without difficulties. You will have to think more carefully about his education and meet his health care needs and he will probably need to stay under your care for a lot longer than most other children. You will also have to plan for his adulthood in a way that most other parents don't have to think about.

You can greatly improve your child's life chances by enabling him to access an appropriate education that fully meets any special educational needs that he may have. Somewhere, you are going to need to find the strength for this fight if your child is going to reach his potential. If your position is less than accepting, you must find a way of putting your anger, grief, or whatever else you may be feeling to one side, so that you can focus on how best to help your child. It may be useful to get support in this from your GP, a counsellor, or from the specialist support organisations that exist to help parents. Some examples of these are The National Autistic Society, The Dyspraxia Foundation, and Contact A Family. Contact details are in the Useful Organisations and Web Resources section at the end of this book.

Once the decision is taken to find out if a diagnosis is appropriate, it is important to bear in mind that although nobody likes to feel their child is labelled, the current system for meeting special educational needs favours those who have a diagnosis. It will also help teachers know how to teach your child. Also bear in mind that it can take a lot of observation and assessment to make a diagnosis. Both of our children have at various times had the appearance of being bright cheerful children, whenever they had appointments with doctors and therapists. They did not present as being severely disabled in the same way as say, a child in a wheelchair might have appeared. Disability takes on many faces, and some disabilities are not so clear at the outset, only becoming more obvious over time.

For us, it was obvious that our children could only benefit from a diagnosis as our efforts to get their school to listen to our concerns about their development and their learning were clearly falling on deaf ears. My own view is that if a child is happy and is achieving at school, then a diagnosis only offers limited benefit. I have yet to meet a struggling and unhappy child for whom life does not get immediately easier, once an appropriate diagnosis is obtained and that information shared with all concerned.

It has also been a good thing for our children to know about their own diagnoses. William was hugely relieved to know he had something which made his speech difficult to understand for the people at nursery school and that this, rather than any other reason, was why they did not seem to do the things he asked for when he was there. Peter was very relieved to understand why he had problems making friends at school and why he frequently found it hard to understand what people meant when they spoke to him. We came to terms quite quickly with our children's diagnoses and welcomed them because we had had to wait so long for the clarity that comes with a diagnosis. Very soon we were saying to each other 'now we know what to do', rather than 'what will we do?' In this way it was very empowering for the whole family.

Once your child is diagnosed, read everything you can lay your hands on about the condition that your child has, and pass on information to school. Talk to friends and relatives and accept any offers of help that are forthcoming. The internet has opened up the world and you will be able to find online resources, forums, email lists, and a wealth of written information and telephone helpline numbers to contact if you want support or information. I have put some of these in the Useful Organisations and Web Resources section of my book.

It must be said that some children simply never get a diagnosis, even if their level of difficulty is very evident. I know I have said a lot about the benefits of diagnosis to getting a statement – these are undeniable. However, if your child remains undiagnosed do not despair! There is a lot to be gained simply by using the health and education services to describe your child's difficulties too. Use them in the same way to build evidence for your child to have their needs met at school, just like anyone else.

Guerrilla Tips

- Accept your role as your child's advocate and find out everything you can about your child's condition and the special educational needs system that will meet them.
- Expect to be taken seriously, but be unstintingly polite in your communications with doctors, therapists, teachers and other professionals.
- Early intervention is the key to overcoming special educational needs.
- Accurate and timely diagnosis of difficulties is vital to children overcoming special educational needs.
- If a doctor tells you that you should adopt a 'wait and see' approach, seek a second opinion – your chances of helping your child recover from his difficulty may diminish over time.
- View any diagnosis as a signpost to light the way for your child, rather than as a label that might stigmatise him.
- Be positive! Keep going until you are happy your child has what he needs to be successful at school.

Within the NHS, we don't often get to nominate a particular doctor or medical professional for our children. If they need a referral, one is made by, say, our GP and the child duly sees a relevant doctor. We are almost conditioned into accepting the doctor we are given. In any other transaction, whether it is going to the dentist, buying a car, taking music lessons, we consider how we feel about the person with whom we are doing business, if they are acting in our best interests, if they are honest and if we are able to work well with them. It is worth applying the same criteria to your child's doctor, especially if the discussion isn't going where you think it should. If you have discussed a diagnosis with your child's doctor but one isn't forthcoming and you feel he needs one, it is worth considering whether you have confidence in the doctor or medical professionals treating your child. What benefits might a diagnosis bring to your child? Think about the educational help your child might be able to access with a diagnosis. If we are unhappy with the way a doctor or medical professional has dealt with our child, it is possible to ask for a second opinion.

If a diagnosis has been made, consider whether it tells the whole story or are you left wondering about other issues your child might have? Sometimes it is simply difficult to diagnose a child, and many never receive a formal diagnosis of their difficulties. If you are confident in your child's current doctor or medical professionals and his needs are being met with or without a diagnosis, there is probably little to be added to the picture. If he lacks a diagnosis, however, and his needs are *not* being met, then it may well be appropriate to seek a second opinion. There have been a number of occasions when we felt a second opinion was appropriate to both of our children, and it was through asking for second opinions, both in our own health authority and out of our area that we arrived at our children's diagnoses.

It can feel awkward to ask your child's doctor for a second opinion. What you are actually telling him is that you disagree and you don't think his conclusion is right. In truth we have always found this a bit tricky but do not be daunted. We have a right to ask for a second opinion. This is what happened to us:

When William was five he was thought to have progressed with his speech so much that he could return full time to his mainstream placement and have a period of 'consolidation'. This means that speech therapy was stopped so that he could have a rest from therapy, and have a period of time to put into practice what he had learned and to see how he did. Over the next year we saw no progress at all and were concerned by this. We now know that if children with verbal dyspraxia are to get better their therapy must be maintained until their speech is fully resolved. We went to see William's paediatrician to discuss this and were shocked when she refused point blank to make a further referral. Her attitude was that William had already had a lot of speech therapy. In fact she felt he had had his fair share and we should be glad about the progress he had made. The truth was that he had done well but his speech was by no means fully resolved and we had allowed him to leave the placement on the understanding that appropriate therapy would be reinstated if needed. We decided to ask for a second opinion and asked for an out-of-area referral to an NHS specialist speech centre at Great Ormond Street. The emphasis was on us to prove that William needed the referral so we asked his local speech therapist to support us. We also contacted Great Ormond Street to ask about the referral criteria for the clinic we wanted. It turned out that they would accept referrals from speech therapists as well as doctors, so after gaining some corroboration from her colleagues that William needed the referral, this was duly done. The Great Ormond Street assessment led to William receiving a further four years of continual speech therapy that he would not have had if we had given up.

After years of our local paediatrician not being sure about Peter's diagnoses, he was diagnosed with Asperger Syndrome (and a lot of other things) at Great Ormond Street following our request for an out-of-area referral.

Your local Patient Advice and Liaison Service (PALS) is a good source of help if you want to investigate the possibility of obtaining a second opinion, either through your local health authority or through an out-of-area referral. Consider these points:

- Is your child having difficulties at school?

- Is there an attainment gap between your child and his peers and is it getting wider? If you are not sure about this check the *Special Educational Needs Code of Practice* for guidance (downloadable from the DCSF website).

- Does your child have a diagnosis, or does your child attend regular medical appointments because of concerns about his development?

- Is your child's medical condition, whether diagnosed or not, a barrier to him accessing the curriculum?

- Have any of your child's teachers ever told you that by not having a diagnosis for your child it will be difficult to get a statement?

- Are you confident that your child's doctor has done all he can to find the correct diagnosis for your child?

- Has your child's school said that it needs more funding to provide all the help your child needs at school?

- Do you consider that your child's school understands his needs and can teach him effectively with the resources it currently has?

- Has any member of staff ever expressed concern over how to teach your child, or your child's attainment in school?

These last two questions are in some ways the most important. If either you or your child's school feel you do not understand fully how to help your child, to teach him, and you suspect a medical condition is at the root of the difficulty, then you need to seek more medical information to either rule in or out any condition that might be affecting your child.

HOW TO GET HELP THROUGH THE PATIENT ADVICE AND LIAISON SERVICE

If you have a concern or a complaint about medical services that your child has received, it is possible to get things resolved through your local PALS office. They can help with problems with your child's medical provision, difficulty getting through to clinics on the telephone, and difficulty obtaining appointments. When using the NHS there are inevitably times when communication is not all it should be and PALS can help to improve matters when communication fails. If your concerns are not resolved when they first intervene they can provide information about making a complaint about the NHS and they can also give advice about getting independent help if you decide you want to do this. We had to go through the procedure of trying to get services locally through PALS before we could reasonably ask for out-of-area referrals. Being able to show that we had first tried to get what the children needed in this way lent credibility to our requests to go to Great Ormond Street Hospital.

CHOOSING THE RIGHT SCHOOL FOR YOUR SPECIAL NEEDS CHILD

By the time children are four or five years old, and about to start school, it is worth asking the head of the nursery or pre-school they are in if they think they are actually ready to start school. Some children with special educational needs benefit from another year in the nursery system at this stage. You most likely won't have a statement in hand at this stage, but if your child is acknowledged as having special needs they may be able to benefit from this. Parents are able to express a preference when nominating a school for their child and if any choice at all is possible where you live make the most of it. This is a partnership that has to work. If you get this wrong it may be difficult for your child to make the change later. It may be that the local school is appropriate for your child but a school must be chosen because it is a good fit, not because it is close by. However, many parents only have a limited choice of schools and it is worth remembering that if your child has a statement this will confer some opportunity to have a say in where your child will go to school. I will talk about this later.

Guerrilla Tips

- If you think your child may have special educational needs, choose their school very carefully if you can.
- The best school for your child may not be the local one. Visit all the ones your child may be eligible to join and check them out carefully. Try to meet parents of other children with similar needs as your son or daughter and find out what they have to say about a range of schools in your area.
- Remember, the school with the best league table scores might not necessarily be the best one for your child. Some lower scoring schools may by necessity have very good provision for children with special educational needs.
- Read all the advice you can lay your hands on about choosing the right school for your child.

Remember the Guerrilla Mum Mantra: Don't take no for an answer, never give up. If in doubt, telephone, email and write letters.

We made huge mistakes over choosing our children's primary school. We bowed to pressure to send them to the local school without looking into it very much at all and this was the source of so much distress. Once there, Peter became attached to his school, simply because it was familiar and he knew what to expect. When problems developed that might have prompted a move, he was very upset at the thought of changing schools, even when school was difficult for him. It is not easy for an autistic child to change schools, and we had no guarantee that it would have been better at any of the other primary schools near us. It was simply not an option to uproot him and head off to another school with no knowledge that it would be any better. Children can quite easily find themselves moving from one school to another in this way becoming more unsettled and more aware of a sense of failure with each move. In any case, when things went wrong for Peter at school we felt that the remedy for this was to put in place the right support for this special educational needs rather than to simply move him to a school that would hopefully (fingers crossed!) meet his needs.

Before your child starts school, obtain a number of school prospectuses from any schools that interest you. You are entitled to visit a school first and to meet with the head and the teacher likely to teach your child. Bear in mind this is an opportunity to see if the school is a good fit for your child and if the head teacher is someone you can work with. Ask lots of questions about how special educational needs are met in the school. Through using small groups? Are children pulled out of classes to do them and if so what will they miss? Do they have mentoring schemes? Ask to see their anti-bullying policy. Ask about the number of exclusions. What is their approach to discipline? How many children in the school have statements? Write down all the questions you can think of to ask and take them with you.

Some parents who think their children will benefit from the smaller class sizes choose to send their children to a small private school. This can work out well for some children, particularly if their needs are not too severe. However, this is not a choice that is open to very many parents – especially in the days of the credit crunch! Some children have places in independent special schools funded by local education authorities under the terms of their statement. I know of a few children in this kind of placement.

If you feel that school is not the right option for your child, then you are entitled to educate him at home. The law states that from the term in which they turn five, all children must receive a formal education, either at school or otherwise. Many families choose to home educate, and there is a thriving online community of people who choose to home educate their special needs children. There are also increasing numbers of home educators' groups which meet regularly and often carry out projects collaboratively. Your LEA will give information about this, and you can also obtain advice from Education Otherwise or other home education support groups. Contact details are in my Useful Organisations and Web Resources section.

In making the most of both the educational and health services available to all children, parents can look ahead to build the case for their children to have their needs identified and met in mainstream education.

Checklist

✳ Make a positive choice to have any special needs your child might have identified and met.

✳ Make the most of the medical services available to you by talking things through with your GP or health visitor to obtain appropriate medical and educational referrals.

✳ When you attend meetings take notes or have someone come with you as note taker. Store your notes and any reports in a place where they will be easily accessible to you.

✳ Actively pursue a diagnosis if you think one is indicated and that this will help your child at school

✳ Get help from PALS or other support organisations if you need it.

This book will give readers an insight into what they are up against – something we only realised when Peter was almost six. I want readers to use our experiences to fight more effectively for their children.

Chapter 2

ASSESSMENT AND PROVISION FOR SPECIAL EDUCATIONAL NEEDS

Getting an Appropriate Mainstream Education for Your Child

WHEN YOUR CHILD GOES TO SCHOOL

In an ideal world, you will have read Chapter 1 and will be at the point of your child starting school, with evidence of any special educational need in hand. If they don't yet have a statement, you will have all the information in place to prevent your child from failing. Sadly, this will not usually be the case. Most parents likely to come across this book will already have had the experience of watching their child struggle at school, and will be at some stage along the road of wondering exactly why the help their child needs seems so elusive. Resources do exist to support children with special educational needs. In principle schools and LEAs are obliged to meet all children's needs. However, if we as parents are to secure some of these resources for our own special needs children, we need to learn how to request them effectively.

I am going to talk about the law in this chapter and how it applies to the services that will support children in mainstream schools with special educational needs. As previously stated, this law applies to England and Wales. If you live in Northern Ireland or Scotland different law applies. Look in my Useful Organisations and Web Resources section for details of organisations that can give information about the law in these places.

Even though different legal systems will apply depending on where you live in the UK, some things are the same wherever you live: to get the school and local education authority to identify a child's level of need and to meet those needs it can be necessary to display a certain level of understanding of the law and the LEA and health services' obligations to your child. If these service providers understand that you know what your child is entitled to receive in terms of services, your child is much more likely to get them. If parents attending school meetings are obviously uninformed about what their child is entitled to, I believe they are less likely to be successful. It pays to do your research so that you can discuss your child's needs on a more level playing field.

A motivated and informed parent can be a successful advocate for their child. It is even possible to access a certain amount of legal advice through free parent support and information services to enable you to argue your child's case. Don't get me wrong, if I felt my child needed something that could only be accessed through a solicitor I would not hesitate to engage one, if I could afford it. My point is that parents do feel disempowered by a system seemingly designed to make them feel ill at ease when navigating it and it is very easy to give up when you feel like this. This is particularly the case at the beginning of the struggle, when parents are at their most vulnerable and ill-informed – and when it is in many ways critical to get the right help. This system gives advantage to those already working within it – teachers, doctors, and LEA officials. Parents new to this are frequently overwhelmed and can feel at a loss as to what they can do to help their child at school. If the school decides to tell them there is no further help available to their child, or that their child does not need more help there is nothing they can say or do to challenge this.

The *Education Act 1996* exists to help children gain an appropriate education. The special educational needs system is underpinned by this law. Although parents do not need to be experts, it will greatly help their case to develop some understanding of this law, and an understanding of how the system works and who to approach when trying to solve problems.

Guerrilla Tips

- Do not be intimidated by your child's school, LEA or health service providers because they know the law, relevant policies, or anything else that you don't know. These things can all be learned by parents too!

- Remain calm and give yourself time to research and learn the things you need to know.

- Access parent advice services and any free legal advice you can – a list of relevant organisations is provided in the Useful Organisations and Web Resources section.

- It helps if you have access to a computer. If you don't have one at home, many libraries have them now, and some charities sell reconditioned computers with obvious savings there.

- If you have access to a computer, join online communities that relate to your child's condition(s). It really is good to talk and these email lists are often hotbeds of good advice and information.

- Read through this book and others like it. A library is the best place to access a lot at a time! The cost can mount up otherwise.

- If they have the resources, some advocacy or parent support groups may help parents fight their case by writing letters, etc. Parents may find they are eligible for this kind of help with some organisations if they are a lone parent, have difficulty understanding the SEN process or are otherwise under stress.

- Try not to panic. I too am prone to panicking, particularly when faced with a new educational problem. It really doesn't help!

THE *EDUCATION ACT 1996*: HOW SPECIAL EDUCATIONAL NEEDS ARE DEFINED

Special educational needs have a legal definition. Whether or not your child fits the definition as having special educational needs under this law will dictate whether the school is obliged to put in extra resources towards meeting their needs.

In law, the *Education Act 1996* defines children with special educational needs as follows:

(1) A child has 'special educational needs' for the purposes of the Act if he has a learning difficulty which calls for special educational provision to be made for him.

(2) Subject to subsection (3) a child has a 'learning difficulty' for the purposes of this Act if –

(a) he has a significantly greater difficulty in learning than the majority of children his age

(b) he has a disability which either prevents or hinders him from making use of educational facilities of a kind generally provided for children of his age in schools within the area of the local education authority *or*

(c) he is under compulsory school age and is, or would be, if special educational provision were not made for him, likely to fall within paragraph (a) or (b) when of that age.

(Education Act 1996, Sections 312 to 336A, Schedule 26 and Schedule 27)

Under the terms of this Act a child cannot be defined as having special educational needs because of reasons caused by the fact that he is speaking English as a second language at school.

Parents may find out that their child has special educational needs when their child is put on the Special Educational Needs Register (SENR) and given an Individual Education Plan (IEP) by the school to help him overcome his special educational needs. The school has to inform parents when they take these measures to help a child. However, parents need not wait for this step to be taken to find out if their child has special educational needs. If parents feel that their child falls into the category of having special educational needs they can take a first step by asking the school to discuss matters with them, and can prompt the school to give their child extra help in class under the terms of an IEP. If only a relatively small amount of help is needed, this can often be funded from the school's own resources. Any support is likely to be given in the context of group work with other children or limited amounts of time spent working one-to-one with a teaching assistant (TA). If you want to take this initial step, begin by discussing matters with your child's teacher.

Most children with special educational needs can be accommodated in a normal classroom, and within the resources the school has at its disposal, although the school may call in a range of health and education specialists to advise them on how to teach the child.

Some good starting points for finding out the basic essentials are:

- The *SEN Code of Practice*, available from the Department for Children, Schools and Families. This is an essential publication. It is downloadable from the DCSF website.

- The *Education Act 1996* and Part IV of the *Disability Discrimination Act 2001* – download copies from the Office for Public Sector Information website.

- *Special Educational Needs (SEN): A Guide for Parents and Carers*. This is also downloadable from the DCSF website.

- The *SEN Toolkit*, available from the Department for Children, Schools and Families. This is the documentation schools should refer to when writing statements.

- There are of course other things to learn about, but these are good starting points. Don't worry, you only need to focus on the things that apply to your child. Details of the relevant websites are in the Useful Organisations and Web Resources section at the end of the book.

Parent support groups are also a really useful resource. Find out about the ones that are relevant to your child. Use their helplines. They are manned by wonderful people with a wealth of experience to share. Whatever your education problem, they will be able to support you or will know someone who can.

THE SPECIAL EDUCATIONAL NEEDS CODE OF PRACTICE

The *SEN Code of Practice* is essential reading for the parent of a child with special educational needs. The reason for this is contained in the foreword: 'it provides practical advice to local education authorities, maintained schools, early education settings and others on carrying out their statutory duties to identify, assess and make provision for children's special educational needs.' Put bluntly, this is the publication that the school and the LEA will be using (or not), in deciding how much, and what kind of help your child may have in school. So how do we decipher this code? There is such a lot of information contained in it. For a very long time I was not at all comfortable with picking out which bits related to my own children's problems because I worried I

Guerrilla Tips

- Do not assume that if your child is struggling at school, you will necessarily be told.
- Look at the legal definition of SEN in the *Education Act 1996* (see above) and decide if your child fits it.
- Expect that you may need to bring up any problems your child may be having yourself.
- Expect that you may need to prompt your child's school to give your child extra help in class.
- Accept that your child's school may well give a certain amount of help to your child with special needs – but only up to a point. They will be watching the pennies!
- Be ready to fight for your child's right to access the curriculum by getting help that costs more money – referrals to Educational Psychologists, specialist teaching services, statutory assessment.
- It is very much to your child's school's advantage if you do not know what you are doing, what your child is entitled to and do not know the law. Inform yourself!
- You can start finding out about your child's condition(s), education law and what you can do to help your child.
- If the school does all of the above for you and seems to bring a suitable solution to your child's problems to you on a plate, be aware that this is a very rare occurrence indeed.

Remember the Guerrilla Mum Mantra: Don't take no for an answer, never give up. If in doubt, telephone, email and write letters.

would get it wrong. I thought I needed someone professional to tell me what to do. Parents can get help in using the code of practice from parent support organisations for as long as they need the support. My need for this kind of support changed as my confidence in using the code of practice increased. We do need to be comfortable with the *SEN Code of Practice.* It is the code we have to use to fight for the help our child needs. It is a bit of a double edged sword, really, because while it can be used to support children obtaining the help they need, it can also be used to justify denying help to children. It is our job to find ways of using it to defend our children's rights. There isn't anything else, and won't be until government comes up with an alternative system.

There are some parts of the *SEN Code of Practice* that I have found to be of great use. I read the sections such as 'Monitoring Pupil Progress' and the part on the stages of 'School Action', 'School Action Plus' and 'Statutory Assessment' and I realised that I could prove my children's need for statutory assessments. For as long as we had remained ignorant of these sections and the *SEN Code of Practice* in general, it had been very easy for the school to fob us off at meetings. If we did not show how applying the *SEN Code of Practice* could improve our sons' situations, the school, or rather the head teacher of the school at that time, was not going to do this either. Later, I found it useful to focus on some key sections and to quote them often in my dealings with teachers and LEA officials. For example, regarding the statutory assessment of special educational needs the *SEN Code of Practice* (DCSF 2001a, p.74) states:

> LEAs must identify and make a statutory assessment of those children for whom they are responsible who have special educational needs and who probably need a statement.
>
> (*Education Act 1996*, Sections 321 and 323)

The Graduated Response – from School Action, to School Action Plus to statutory assessment

The Graduated Response is a series of steps laid out in the *SEN Code of Practice* designed to provide a framework for school-based intervention. It begins with an initial differentiated curriculum in the area(s) of difficulty. If very little or no progress is seen, the child is put on to School Action and the child receives extra help within the school. Any measures the school takes to support a child are written down in an IEP and these should be reviewed by the school regularly. This is an action plan showing how your child's teacher is going to give your child extra help in class and how it will be determined if this has been effective. If this does not help, then the child is moved up to the next stage of the process, School Action Plus. The *SEN Code of Practice* (DCSF 2001a, p.52, Section 5:43) states that:

When a class teacher or the SENCO identifies a child with SEN the class teacher should provide interventions that are <u>additional to</u> or <u>different from</u> those provided as part of the school's usual differentiated curriculum offer and strategies (School Action).

Section 5:44 then goes into more detail, stating that:

The triggers for intervention through School Action could be the teacher's or others' concern, underpinned by evidence, about a child who despite receiving differentiated learning opportunities:

- makes little or no progress even when teaching approaches are targeted particularly in a child's identified areas of weakness

- shows signs of difficulty in developing literacy or mathematics skills which result in poor attainment in some curriculum areas

- presents persistent emotional or behavioural difficulties which are not ameliorated by the behaviour management techniques usually employed in the school

- has sensory or physical problems, and continues to make little or no progress despite the provision of specialist equipment

- has communication and/or interaction difficulties, and continues to make little or no progress despite the provision of a differentiated curriculum.

(DCSF 2001a, pp.52–53)

Before placing a child onto a School Action the teacher and SENCO are already likely to have tried a differentiated curriculum. The next level of intervention is School Action, where the child is likely to receive access to special group work or individual support. If progress is still not seen through School Action interventions, such as group work with a TA, a child may progress to School Action Plus. There is an expectation that the child will then begin to receive more sustained input from services outside the school, such as occupational therapy services, literacy support services and so on. The *SEN Code of Practice* (DCSF 2001a, p.54, Section 5:54) states:

A request for help from external services is likely to follow a decision taken by the SENCO and colleagues, in consultation with parents, at a meeting to review the child's IEP. Schools should always consult specialists when they take action on behalf of a child through School Action Plus. But the involvement of specialists need not be limited to such children. Outside specialists can play an important part in the very early identification of special educational needs and in advising schools on effective provision designed to prevent the development of more significant needs. They can act as consultants and be a source of in-service advice on learning and behaviour management strategies for all teachers.

Chapter 5 of the *SEN Code of Practice* goes into more detail about accessing help through the Graduated Response in the primary phase and Chapter 6 is about the Graduated Response in secondary education.

Guerrilla Tips

- Many children who have special educational needs are well supported, and can progress well without a statement. If your child is one of these, no further action is necessary.

- If an education or health professional tells you that your child can't have something, whether that is a statement or anything else, make it your business to find out from an independent source if it is true.

- If you think your child is struggling significantly at school, is not making adequate progress and you think they need a statement, don't be afraid to say so and don't be put off, especially if teachers disagree but cannot give you good reasons for that.

- Remember if a child's needs *are* met in school, he *will* progress. If he is *not* well supported, he *will not* progress. It is that simple.

- If you find reading the *SEN Code of Practice* daunting try asking your child's school SENCO for advice in the first instance.

- If you don't get the right advice from this source, ask parent support groups for help.

- Don't give up until you are happy that measures are in place that will support your child well enough for them to progress.

Be certain that if you are told your child does not need a statement, that there are solid reasons behind it, such as that your child has succeeded in closing the attainment gap after an initial differentiated curriculum, and is achieving in line with his peers. Make sure that this process is properly documented.

According to the *SEN Code of Practice*, if your child still fails to progress after benefiting from interventions on School Action and School Action Plus, then a statutory assessment may be considered.

It seems straightforward enough that this process will result in children getting the right type of help in school when they need it. However, it does not always follow that a child will be moved through the stages appropriately. If your child is put on to School Action you should satisfy yourself that this represents the correct level of intervention for their level of difficulty.

Peter was held down by his school on School Action for six years. This is the first level of additional support. When he joined reception class he had already been accessing physiotherapy, speech and language therapy, specialist teachers, occupational therapy among other interventions for three years. These interventions reflected needs which indicated that he should have been accessing a much higher level of support and according to the *SEN Code of Practice* he had long been eligible to be defined on School Action Plus. When we tried to make a case for him to be referred for statutory assessment, the third tier, the school was able to point at the Graduated Response and say that his level of involvement and needs did not indicate that he should have one – because he was still 'only' on School Action!

To be held down for six years on School Action was devastating to Peter's achievement and there was nothing we could do to stop the *SEN Code of Practice* being interpreted in this very limited way. Money and resources can be saved by keeping a child on School Action and not increasing the help they can have. When at a school meeting I asked an LEA officer for her opinion as to whether it was time to progress him to the next level, she supported the school keeping him on School Action. Peter had no effective support for his learning, social or emotional needs until he was in Year 5. The LEA used his apparent lack of progression along this continuum to say that he had not yet triggered a statutory assessment; therefore it was impossible for them to do an assessment.

As you can see, there is plenty of scope for the Graduated Response to be abused. The bottom line, however, is that if you think the attainment gap between your child and his peers is widening, it is very important to take action, as you could well be entitled to more and better service provision. Schools do have to keep detailed records on progress and attainment, and parents can see these records.

The *SEN Code of Practice* has this to say about how attainment in children at school should be measured:

7:40 LEAs should always be alert to indications that a child's learning difficulties may be particularly complex or intractable. They should be alert, therefore, to significant discrepancies between:

- a child's attainments in assessments and tests in core subjects of the National Curriculum and the attainment of the majority of children of their age

- a child's attainments in assessments and tests in core subjects of the National Curriculum and the performance expected of the child as indicated by a consensus among those who have taught and observed the child, including their parents and supported by such standardised tests as can reliably be administered

- a child's attainment within one of the core subjects of the National Curriculum or between one core subject and another

- a child's attainments in early learning goals in comparison with the attainments of the majority of their peers.

7:41 LEAs should therefore seek clear recorded evidence of the child's academic attainment and ask, for example, whether:

- the child is not benefiting from working on programmes of study relevant to the key stage appropriate to their age or from earlier key stages...

- the child is working at a level significantly below that of their contemporaries in any of the core subjects of the National Curriculum or the foundation stage curriculum

- there is evidence that the child is falling progressively behind the majority of children of their age in academic attainment in any of the National Curriculum core subjects, as measured by standardised tests and the teachers' own recorded assessments of a child's classroom work, including any portfolio of the child's work.

(DCSF 2001a, p.82)

If your child has come this far through the Graduated Response and is still having difficulties, you may wish to consider whether he would benefit from having a statutory assessment of his special educational needs. This is the method by which a child's needs are assessed by the LEA. It is a much more certain way of having his needs met at school because LEAs and schools are legally obliged to deliver any provision made through a statement. In attempting to obtain a statutory assessment for a child, it is of vital importance to outline any difficulties in light of his actual levels of attainment at school. It is easy to focus on how difficult a child may find school, and how upset he is. It is more difficult to highlight and prove their lack of progress. You must present clear evidence to the LEA detailing any lack of progress when you ask for statutory assessment. You must be able to show the growing attainment gap between your child and other children in his class in the core subjects and across the curriculum. If you do not it is relatively easy for LEAs to opt out of doing a statutory assessment. LEAs are also required to take into account the following points. Section 7:43 of the *SEN Code of Practice* (DCSF 2001a, p.83) states that LEAs should also consider, 'evidence of any other identifiable factors that could impact on learning outcomes'. These include:

- clear, recorded evidence of clumsiness; significant difficulties of sequencing or visual perception; deficiencies in working memory; or significant delays in language functioning

- any evidence of impaired social interaction or communication or a significantly restricted repertoire of activities, interests and imaginative development

- evidence of significant emotional or behavioural difficulties, as indicated by clear recorded examples of withdrawn or disruptive behaviour; a marked and persistent inability to concentrate; signs that the child experiences considerable frustration or distress in relation to their learning difficulties; difficulties in establishing and maintaining balanced relationships with their fellow pupils or with adults; and any other evidence of a significant delay in the development of life and social skills.

Read the *SEN Code of Practice* thoroughly and learn about the kind of evidence you will need to gather, such as written classroom observations of your child's behaviour, to push the LEA to make a statutory assessment of your child's special educational needs. Some good ways of finding evidence are:

- Read your child's school records. You are entitled to see them although you can't take the originals away with you. You may be asked for a photocopying charge if you want copies.

- Teachers are obliged to keep records of how your child is progressing in school. You do not have to wait until formal testing results, such as SATS results, become available to find out how your child is doing.

- Peruse any Individual Education Plans – if targets are consistently not met, highlight this.

- If, over time, your child continues to fall behind, and does not catch up, and the attainment gap between him and other children in the class gets wider, this is evidence in itself.

- Keep tabs on any recorded evidence of clumsiness, visual processing problems, significant language delays, working memory deficiencies, emotional or behavioural problems, and any sign your child is experiencing a lot of distress or frustration because of his learning difficulties.

If you can present accurate records of the above when you put in your request for a statutory assessment, it makes it more difficult for the LEA to refuse to assess and gives you good grounds for any appeal to the Special Educational Needs and Disability Tribunal.

It was only when we had a good working knowledge of the *SEN Code of Practice* that we started to really make a difference to our children's lives at school. As I keep saying, ask the school for help in learning about the *SEN Code of Practice* and if you need further help the parent support agencies are always more than happy to help you understand it.

LOCAL AUTHORITY CRITERIA REGARDING SPECIAL EDUCATIONAL NEEDS

I have heard a lot about the LEA criteria, usually quoted at me at length to explain why my children would not qualify for things. I used to hear them referred to so often and with such conviction that I really did believe that if the local criteria said my children should not have something, then that was it. When I got into reading the *SEN Code of Practice*, I realised that any local authority criteria relating to how the local education authority deals with identifying and meeting special educational needs must be carried out with absolute regard to the law and the *SEN Code of Practice*, and that any local criteria must not supersede these. Also, blanket policies are banned, for example, 'we don't statement for speech delays/autism/dyslexia'. Any learning needs must be assessed on their own merits and met accordingly. If anyone says too much about 'LEA criteria', 'local criteria', or 'county criteria', or anything that sounds remotely similar, then you must get advice immediately from one of the parent support organisations, or one of the sources of legal advice open to parents. This will help you decide if what you are hearing is relevant to your child's case, or even legal.

WORKING WITH THE SCHOOL AND THE LEA TO MEET YOUR CHILD'S SPECIAL EDUCATIONAL NEEDS

I have at times found it very difficult to be an effective advocate for my children and to remain on good terms with teachers. I always try to start off positively and the teacher or SENCO is always my initial port of call when I have a query. However, I am always keen to see evidence that the school is acting in my child's best interests and I do act if their needs are unmet. It makes for a good deal of conflict. As parents of children with special educational needs we (that is, my husband and I) have to play a very tricky game. We have been through some very rough patches when we felt disappointed or angry in our dealings with teachers and the school. It is extremely difficult to forge positive relationships on this basis and very easy to fall out with teachers. This means that we have to work much harder than other parents to foster positive feelings and good communication. The key to building an effective working partnership with the school is to try very hard to choose the right school in the first place. Know what you are looking for when you visit. Find out how special needs are identified and met, making sure the school is fully engaged in the necessity to get this right. Without asking for specific information about particular children, it will be possible to find out how the school goes about fulfilling its obligations to meet special educational needs. Once you are as certain as you can be that the school can meet your child's needs, and your child has begun to attend the school, ensure that the school has all the relevant information regarding your child's needs such as medical reports, any educational assessments and so on. Do remember to keep any discussion relevant.

Your increasing knowledge of SEN Law and the *SEN Code of Practice* will mark you out as a parent who knows what they are talking about and what your child is entitled to. Don't be afraid to show your knowledge. Those people with your child's future in their hands need to know you mean business!

Now that our children's needs are met in school and we are not the frustrated, angry and afraid parents that we once were, the working relationship we have with our children's school today is much healthier. We are prepared to disagree with teachers and to be full partners with the school in meeting our children's needs. When the school or LEA makes mistakes we request meetings and go through what went wrong. Sometimes the LEA thanks us and makes changes to its systems to prevent similar things happening again. We also make a point of telling teachers and the LEA whenever they get something right and we involve our children in decisions about their education. They have begun to attend annual reviews of their statements and are slowly learning to be their own advocates at school. It may seem a long way away, but if they go to college they will need to be able to speak for themselves and to negotiate their own support for their special educational needs.

Guerrilla Tips

- Always try to start off on the right foot with your child's class teacher or form teacher.

- At the beginning of term make an appointment to meet with him or her, so that you can introduce yourself, if it is a new teacher, and pass on information about your child's condition. Offer to answer any other questions he or she might have.

- Ask if there is anything you can do, or if there is anything he or she would like to know more about to make it easier for him or her to help your child.

- Make it very easy for her or him to get hold of you by ensuring that contact details are kept up to date with the school office.

- Always have your mobile phone with you when your child is at school.

- Try not to bombard teachers with too many requests for meetings. Use the usual opportunities the school might have, such as parents' evenings and Individual Education Plan meetings to discuss concerns as much as possible. This way, they will know that if you request a meeting, then you really need one.

- There will be times when your child's school or teacher, or even the LEA, disagrees with you and you feel your child is not receiving the help he needs. Do not get angry or allow your feelings to become personal. Be as calm as possible. You may disagree, but your child will be the one who loses out if you do not do all you can to maintain a positive relationship with the school in order to be able to keep talking.

- Remember, maintaining a positive relationship with the school does not mean you have to give in when you have a disagreement. Keep working towards your aim using the law, *SEN Code of Practice* and parent support organisations to support you.

- If you are sure the school is wrong, or is not acting in the best interests of your child, be ready to take positive action to remedy the situation.

- It is up to you to pull together all the relevant information to ensure your child's school has a relevant picture of your child's needs.

SEN FUNDING: SCHOOL-RESOURCED HELP AND STATEMENTED HELP

For over 25 years, children with special educational needs have had the right to have their special educational needs identified, assessed and met. Those with high levels of need can have these met under the terms of a statement of special educational needs. Under the terms of the *Education Act 1996*, local authorities are responsible for ensuring that statemented children receive the help they are entitled to receive through their statements, even if the school fails to provide it.

Without going into too much detail, I would like to outline some important changes that have taken place in recent years that have impacted greatly on how schools fund provision for special educational needs. In 2004, the DfES initiative, *Removing Barriers to Achievement* (a government strategy document setting out how the government intends to give children with special educational needs the opportunity to succeed) outlined the requirement for local authorities to make funds for supporting children with special educational needs much more readily available. In addition to their usual funding, schools would receive an additional payment that could be used to meet the needs of as many children as possible, in a more direct way, and at an earlier stage. It was hoped that this would have the effect of preventing the main body of children with special educational needs that might require a statement, from actually having to go through the statutory assessment process to access funding. In short, the DfES said they wanted children who needed it to access help earlier, but also that they wanted to reduce the number of statements. They decided that schools would receive a 'delegated budget' for SEN. This is a payment made by LEAs to schools to be spent on meeting special educational needs. It is calculated based on points such as the number of children receiving free school meals and social deprivation indicators with the schools ticking the most boxes receiving the highest payments. In principle the effect of this should be to make it easier for children to get help in school and to reduce the number of children needing a statement. It sounds good, doesn't it? However, the key factor in whether or not this approach is a success is in how the individual LEAs apply this new policy and whether the money actually reaches all the children who need it. As a parent of two children with statements, I am immediately suspicious of any policy developed with the purpose of reducing the number of children receiving new statements. It has certainly resulted in fewer statements being issued. It also means that the school is responsible for funding more provision than previously out of its delegated budget.

This move is likely to cause financial difficulties for some schools, particularly those who do not qualify for large delegated funding payments. Perhaps worst of all, it will reduce the number of children whose needs are provided for and protected by a legally binding document – the statement. Parents of children without statements whose needs are not being met at school can only complain to the governors of the school on the basis that they are not using their 'best endeavours' to meet needs, in accordance with Section 317 (a) *Education Act 1996*. This is much shakier ground. If the right to have special educational needs provided for is reduced by fewer statements being issued, children with significant needs will inevitably slip through the net. Also, there is no way of ensuring that the delegated funding to meet special educational needs in schools will be enough to meet the needs of all the children depending on it. Furthermore, there is no way of protecting this money so that it is in fact spent on the children for whom it is intended. If a child's SEN are significant, then a statement is by far the most effective way of protecting their interests.

Where statements are issued, Part 3 of the statement must set out funding arrangements for meeting need. In the light of *Removing Barriers To Achievement* many local authorities have set thresholds relating to the funding of statements, saying that where less than a certain number of hours of support per week is conferred on any child, then this must be met out of the school's delegated funding. They claim that they allow for this in their budgeting. In my area this threshold is set at 15 hours per week, which I believe is not uncommon. Schools must pay for the first 15 hours and then any hours over this number are funded by the LEA. We are lucky because our LEA decided to continue to centrally fund all statements given before 2004 regardless of the number of hours of support given and statements with 15 hours of TA support or less issued before 2004 are still centrally funded. Not all LEAs chose to do this. Where statements attract central funding, schools receive extra payments over and above the general delegated budget for special educational needs from the LEA to fund the statement. However, there is no guarantee that the delegated funding will be enough to meet the needs of all unstatemented children *and* cover all statements that have to be funded by the school – those statements conferring hours of support that fall beneath the threshold set and must be paid for by the school. It is easy to understand how the head teacher of a school might have a hard choice to make if he knows a child probably needs a statement but that his statemented hours of support would be unlikely to meet the threshold, especially if the school is already struggling to fund all the statements that must be funded from its delegated budget. I believe that this policy has also begun to affect schools admissions. When I enquired about a place for William at his secondary school, the first question that was asked about him was whether his statement was centrally funded or not. For schools statements are only a good thing from a financial point of view if they bring more money into the school and are not a financial drain.

Unless your child is likely to attract a certain number of hours in support, your child's school may well be reluctant to support you in getting a statement. Do not let this put you off. Remember, even statements paid for out of the school's delegated funding must be delivered.

Guerrilla Tips

- If your child really needs a statement it is unlikely that delegated funding arrangements will adequately meet his needs on a long term basis.
- Keep copies of all Individual Education Plans and do not be afraid to point out any targets that have not been met.
- Keep track of your child's attainment through school assessment. If the gap between your child's attainment and that of other children is widening, accept this as an alarm bell and do not be afraid to push for a statement.
- You can now see why schools may not favour statutory assessment as a means to meeting special educational needs. Accept that some parents will have to request statutory assessment without the support of the school. If you are one of those parents do not be too afraid to try.

SPECIALIST EDUCATION AND HEALTH-BASED SUPPORT SERVICES YOUR CHILD MAY ACCESS THROUGH THE SCHOOL'S OWN RESOURCES

Schools have a responsibility to provide a differentiated curriculum to any child requiring it, although this intervention is on its own unlikely to meet the needs of children requiring statutory assessment. So what specialist education and health-based support services can these children access through the school's own resources? There are a number of specialist teaching services that schools may use for the benefit of their pupils. As ever, resources are limited and you may well have to put considerable effort into negotiating with the school, compiling educational reports, and proving your child's lack of progress to access it. To be honest, if you are doing all of this you might as well be trying to get a statement. Nevertheless, children at School Action and School Action Plus may benefit from these services.

You are much more likely to be able to access them for your child if you know that they exist! Good sources of information about what is available are your child's school – also ask the SENCO, the local Parent Partnership Service, the Student Assessment Office, and other parents! Our children have been able to benefit from a range of services and not all of them have depended on them having a statement.

Literacy programmes

Literacy programmes focus on ensuring that children develop reading and writing skills. Our children have been able to learn to read but have had huge difficulty with writing. There comes a point at which the usual occupational therapy interventions simply do not support handwriting development enough, and handwriting issues remain. As a result of a discussion between ourselves and the SENCO, our children have, alongside other classmates, accessed a handwriting programme through the school. For our children, this offered limited success, and indicated a need for an IT-based intervention. Further discussions with the school led to the school purchasing typing programmes. The licence purchased enabled both of our children and others in the school to have the opportunity to learn to type to support poor handwriting skills and to enable them to record their own work. This eventually led to our children having their own IT needs written into their statements when they got them and they now have their own laptops. Having laptops under the terms of their statements, they can use the typing programmes at home as well as at school, and they can independently complete homework whereas other children who do not have statements but who use laptops at school only have access to laptops at school.

Educational psychologist

Parents often know that an educational psychology report forms a part of a statutory assessment but many do not realise that they can be called in by the school to assess any child experiencing difficulties. The barrier to this is that it costs the school money to do this. In fairness, there is a continuum of measures a school may take to help any child that they may wish to access first before paying for this service. If, after trying other things, they then think that a child needs to be assessed by an educational psychologist, my view is that they should be supporting the parents in an attempt to obtain a statutory assessment too.

Information technology

Many schools have a wide range of IT supports in place for all children to access. In terms of recording work, access to appropriate IT support has been vital for both of my children, as they simply cannot do enough handwriting to fully support the work they are capable of achieving. It is well worth getting to know the IT policy at your child's school to get an idea of the level of support you can expect. Once that is established you may begin to think about additional support you may wish to try to obtain and if a statement might be appropriate.

Health services

Occupational therapists, physiotherapists and speech therapists have all been very active in supporting our children in school. It is possible to self-refer for some health services. If you think your child might benefit from accessing these services, it is worth asking your GP or paediatrician for information about how to obtain a referral. The school can also make referrals, but sometimes schools can be very slow in getting around to actually making referrals. These therapists have attended many meetings about our children at school, both before and after they got their statements and are very useful in devising Individual Education Plans to be carried out in the classroom.

Teaching assistant support

Many classes have teaching assistants attached to them in order to provide help to a range of children. This help is limited, and is often carried out in group work activities. Some children can access enough help to meet their needs in this way but there are many children who are simply not adequately supported by this level of help.

There may well be other services available. The best people to ask are at your child's school or in the local education authority. They will be able to give a comprehensive overview of the services available where you live. If they are not helpful, seek advice from a parent support organisation.

WHERE TO GET GOOD, OBJECTIVE AND FREE ADVICE ABOUT YOUR CHILD

It can be very daunting to realise that your child has special educational needs and that as their parent it is up to you to do all you can to access specialist services on their behalf. We felt isolated and powerless, and our level of worry about our child was permanently high. It helped a great deal to talk to another parent who was a seasoned fighter and to find that our concerns were valid, had to be acted upon and that it was not unusual for schools to take the tack Peter's was, in an effort not to spend money on individual children and blow the budget. The more we talked to parents, the more we realised that we were having a common experience. We also realised that this is the point at which many give up and don't fight on because the task can seem impossible. Once we felt more empowered that was a turning point. We got on the internet and began to research the difficulties Peter had. It was a revelation to find out about the existence of organisations like the Independent Panel for Special Educational Advice, the National Autistic Society, the Dyspraxia Foundation, and others, all of whom offer free, expert advice through their telephone helplines.

Checklist

∗ Know your stuff – get to know the contents of the *SEN Code of Practice* and the *Education Act 1996*.

∗ Does your child have special educational needs under the terms of the *Education Act 1996*?

∗ If so, read about the Graduated Response and the triggers for statutory assessment.

∗ Develop a good working relationship with your child's teachers and school.

∗ Learn about special educational needs funding.

∗ Find out what your child is entitled to receive through the delegated special needs budget.

∗ Find out about educational and health services that can be brought in by the school to help your child access the curriculum.

∗ Don't be afraid to say so when you think your child's school has helped your child all it can from its own resources and look toward statutory assessment to meet your child's learning needs.

∗ If you co-ordinate all of the pieces of information and keep the school informed of the outcome of appointments, they will be in a much better position to teach your child.

Chapter 3

THE STATUTORY
ASSESSMENT PROCESS

WHEN THE SCHOOL CAN DO NO MORE WITHOUT ADDITIONAL FUNDING FROM THE LEA

It was not immediately apparent to us that the school had reached the point at which it could do no more for our children without additional funding. We did not have access to our children's school records because we did not know that we had the right to see them and did not ask. Nor did any teacher tell us that this point had been reached until we specifically asked them – and then only after considerable wrangling. Some parents may be lucky enough to have their child in a school which first broaches the subject of statutory assessment with them, but we were not lucky enough to be in this position. However the information comes out, the school should be able to give you evidence of how your child is doing in terms of attainment and whether their school-based strategies to help your child are working. If they are not working and the school can do no more, then ask if they will support you in getting a statutory assessment of your child's special educational needs. If the school proves unwilling to make the referral, however, there is provision in the *Education Act 1996* under Sections 328 and 329, for parents to do it themselves.

An important point to keep in mind is that the *SEN Code of Practice* does say that the Graduated Response should not be seen as hoops to jump through before a referral for statutory assessment may be made. A child may be referred at any time if their level of difficulty at school warrants this.

Guerrilla Tips

The statutory assessment process is the only way to be sure your child's needs will be met.

🐾 It is important that parents understand the Graduated Response – look it up in the *SEN Code of Practice* (DCSF 2001a, pp.33–34, 38, 48)

🐾 Read it and become really familiar with it.

🐾 Decide how it might apply to your child's case.

🐾 Do not assume that the school will be doing this. You will quite likely have to fight hard to get them to progress your child through these stages as they ought to do.

🐾 Be prepared to fight for your child's case!

🐾 Most children on the special needs register will be accessing help either through School Action or School Action Plus. There are marked differences between these stages. Read about these levels in the *SEN Code of Practice* (pp.35–36, 52–56, 68–72) so you know which one is appropriate to your child's needs.

🐾 Remember it is not essential for a child to have moved through all of these stages to have a statutory assessment although your child's school is likely to want to 'stick' to this.

🐾 Look up 'statutory assessment' in your *SEN Code of Practice* (pp.39–43, 56–58, 74, 95). Does this appear to meet your child's needs?

🐾 As always approach parent support organisations for help if you need it.

Remember the Guerrilla Mum Mantra: Don't take no for an answer, never give up. If in doubt, telephone, email and write letters.

THE STATUTORY ASSESSMENT PROCESS: WHAT IS IT? DOES YOUR CHILD NEED IT?

Statutory assessment is the method used by a LEA to identify a child's special educational needs and to decide what provision to make for them. If an agreement is made to assess a child then a statement of special educational needs may result from these investigations.

The *SEN Code of Practice* (DCSF 2001a) states that 'LEAs must identify and make a statutory assessment of those children for whom they are responsible who have special educational needs and who probably need a statement. See Sections 321 and 323, *Education Act*

1996.' Schools can, of course, make referrals, and so can parents. I think it is best to do the referral yourself because not only do you retain control of proceedings, because all correspondence will be sent to you, the parent, not the school, but you will also know the referral has been done and are switched on about timescales and so on, which are important. If your school wants to help, perhaps they can write a letter of support for you to include in your referral. Your letter to the LEA might follow the template I provide below.

Dear Sir or Madam,

(Child's name and date of birth)

I am the parent of (child's name and date of birth). I am writing to you to request that you conduct an assessment of his (or her) special educational needs under Section 323 of the *Education Act 1996*.

(Child's name) attends . . . . school.

I believe that (child's name)'s special educational needs are as follows:

. . . .

. . . .

. . . .

I do not believe that (child's name)'s school can on their own make the provision to meet his (or her) special educational needs. My reasons for this are as follows:

. . . .

. . . .

. . . .

I enclose the following reports. They are: (list reports, i.e. occupational therapy report (date) and name of author).

I understand that you are required by law to reply to this request within six weeks and that if you refuse I will have the right to appeal to the Special Educational Needs Tribunal.

Yours faithfully

(Your name)

Parents might decide to refer a child for statutory assessment following a period of time spent within the Graduated Response process with little or no progress, or because they think that their child's level of need is severe enough to warrant immediate referral for statutory assessment without going through the Graduated Response.

There is a set timescale that the LEA must follow in deciding whether to make a statement. By law it must take no more than six weeks from start to finish, and they have to have very good reasons to break these time limits. The timescale is as follows.

Statutory assessment timescale

- *Six weeks* – Six weeks in which to receive a request for statutory assessment and to decide whether they are going to make that assessment. At the end of six weeks they have to make the decision to assess or not to assess your child, and to tell you of that decision in writing.

- *Ten weeks* – A further ten weeks in which to seek and receive advice from all the relevant parties involved in the care and education of your child. This means the school, occupational therapists, physiotherapists, speech therapists, educational psychologists, paediatrician, parents and any other medical or education professional. At this point they have to decide whether they are going to make a proposed statement for your child or not make a statement.

- *Two weeks* – A further two weeks after finishing the assessment of your child to prepare the proposed statement and send it to you or to tell you that they are not going to issue a statement and to send you a note in lieu, which is a letter telling you what they think your child's needs are and how they recommend the school uses its resources to meet those needs.

- *Eight weeks* – If a proposed statement is made, parents will receive a copy and will be asked to sign and return a form within fifteen days saying if they agree with the proposed statement. The LEA must make the statement final within eight weeks. For us, this is a time in which emails fly thick and fast between us and the LEA as we negotiate the wording of the statement and clarify issues through discussion with the professionals consulted during the assessment. The statement is then made final and becomes a legally binding document.

The total time you can expect this process to take therefore is around six months.

If the LEA agrees to carry out an assessment of your child's needs and then decides *not* to issue a statement, saying that he doesn't need one, they will write a report detailing what they think your child's needs are and how they should be met out of the school's budget. This is the 'note in lieu'. These are not really worth very much because the school does not legally have to follow them and is probably doing all it can with the funding it has anyway.

If you are not happy with the proposed statement you may ask in writing and within fifteen days of the date on the letter, for a meeting with the officer named on the letter to discuss your concerns. They also have to inform you of local mediation or conciliation services such as the Parent Partnership Service and often, even if parents are initially unhappy with the proposed statement, differences can be resolved through these methods. We prefer to go direct to the LEA officers involved to discuss matters with them on a one-to-one basis. Even if we don't actually have a face-to-face meeting we can often get changes agreed through email correspondence.

Your child should come out of this process with a statement you are happy with and which will support his needs in school. If the LEA refuses to assess, to issue a statement, or if you do not agree with the final document, then you have the right to make an appeal to the First-tier Tribunal (Special Educational Needs and Disability). This is a government body set up to settle these disputes and their decision is legally binding. In some circumstances it is possible to appeal their decisions.

This all appears to be very straightforward. It should be, but it isn't. It is common for children to be refused a statutory assessment even when they fit the criteria.

As parents it can be difficult to come to terms with the necessity to fight for your child. Even with the letter of refusal on the table in front of us, telling us that we could appeal to the Tribunal if we disagreed with the decision, somehow it did not seem possible to appeal, or appropriate to complain, to make waves, to do anything that we feared would impact negatively on our children. We did not want to upset the school or make the education officers even less willing to help us. We were doormats despite Peter's and William's obvious needs, and at times we found ourselves 'keeping the peace' with school to their cost. It was the cause of so much stress and despair in our house as we strove to decide what to do.

Guerrilla Tips

Here are the key points to remember about the statutory assessment process.

- Remember that legislation is already in place to ensure that children receive the support that they need for their special educational needs.

- Whether this step is taken depends on someone initiating the process. Very often this must be the parents.

- Remember that there is a potential conflict of interest in that the LEAs decide on what help to give a child *but* they manage the budgets too! They have financial targets to meet and budget cuts to work around. It is in their best interests to spend as little money as possible and they will do all they can to try to achieve this aim.

- You will encounter disagreements, incompetence and on occasion duplicity. You probably won't get what you want for your child straight away – so start early!

- You will cope better with all of these things if you have done your research and know your child's rights.

- You will also encounter people who genuinely want to help, even in the LEA.

- Remember that even when you are angry, do not lose your temper when speaking with anyone involved in identifying and meeting your child's needs. There are mediation services within the LEA you can use, and it is always worth trying to negotiate. It is in the LEA's interest to resolve differences without having to go to tribunals or answer other official complaints.

WHAT TO PUT IN YOUR PARENTS' REPORT

Once you have sent off your letter of referral, the statutory assessment process begins. You will receive a letter and information pack detailing how this process will unfold. Hopefully by the time that a statutory assessment is requested for their child, parents will have a lot of educational and medical information in the form of written reports about their child. The LEA will ask all of the medical and educational professionals whom your child has seen about your child and about what they think they need to be able to access the curriculum and progress in school. Make sure the LEA has a list from you of all the people who have assessed and written reports about your child. They can't ask them for information if they don't know who they are! So email them, ring them up or write to your special needs officer (SNO) to tell them. The SNO is the person from the LEA who will correspond with you and keep you up to date with what is happening. Parents are also invited to give their views and the child's own thoughts about school are canvassed. I always find it tremendously difficult to do a good parents' report because my views are coloured by my feelings. However, this is your one chance to say something to the panel that they have to consider alongside all of the other evidence, so it is worth spending some time on it. The information pack you receive from the LEA will tell you what it wants you to cover. When I look back on our unsuccessful attempts to obtain statements, the emphasis of my parental report was really quite emotional. By the time of our successful bid to get Peter statemented, I had learned not to do this.

Guerrilla Tips

- Include the main underlying conditions – for example, dyslexia, dyspraxia, autism, vision impairment, attention difficulties, ADHD.
- Show how the conditions prevent your child accessing the curriculum.
- Consider your child's development in the core skills, particularly literacy. If a child cannot read he is prevented almost by default from accessing most of the curriculum.
- Think about specialist teaching services that might benefit your child and say why you think these will help. Refer back to Chapter 2 if you are not sure what these might be. Ask your child's SENCO about what is available to children with special educational needs in your area, both with and without a statement.

- Focus on any attainment gaps between your child and his peers in all areas of the curriculum.

- Focus on any sensory or physical difficulties and how they impact on your child at school. For example, hearing problems (glue ear?), fine motor skill development, ligament laxity or hypotonia. Can your child sit still and pay attention to the teacher, or stay on task or hold a pencil? Can he participate in PE?

- Does your child have any mobility issues that prevent him accessing the curriculum or using the school's facilities in the same way as other children?

- Consider any equipment your child may need to access the curriculum. For example he may benefit from having a wedge to help sitting posture or laptop for recording work. Does he need any training to use the equipment, for example, typing tuition?

- Ask your child what kind of help he thinks he needs at school.

- Discuss your child's social inclusion at school.

- Discuss any bullying issues.

- Include any therapies the child is currently accessing along with targets. Say whether the targets have been reached.

- Include Individual Education Plans. Say whether the targets on them have been attained. Focus on areas where your child has repeatedly failed. Do not assume the school will necessarily be doing this in their report.

- It is worth mentioning that your child's school may be playing the 'optimism game' and may focus heavily on the things your child can do, or has achieved. This is not helpful so don't be sucked in. Be brutally honest with yourself when you write this report.

- Remember, all of the cases for statutory assessment may well be considered at the same meeting or panel. You are in a competitive environment. Keep your report factual but no issue is too big or small to be included in your report. Make your child's case as compelling as possible.

- Is your child unduly stressed by any difficulty he may be having at school? Is this impacting upon his health or school attendance?

This is your opportunity to have your say, in the hope that your report will be listened to by a panel of people whom you can't meet. You don't know who they are except that they are professionals drawn from a variety of roles in education. It is worth bearing in mind that they have to canvass our opinions but that parents have very little power in these panels. To be listened to, you will need to back up your comments with evidence from the professionals' reports that you will hopefully have already obtained about your child. Your opinions will be harder to refute if backed up by the evidence of other professionals who have written reports on your child. Talk to the authors of your child's reports about what you hope to achieve for your child in having the assessment and tell them you are asking for a statutory assessment. They may be able to think of things to highlight that will help your case. In other words, it helps if you are all singing from the same song sheet!

There is nothing as depressing as having to compile a (usually long) list of all of your child's difficulties and shortcomings. By Year 5 Peter had some support hours in place – although still not enough – and a new head teacher had tried out some different ways of helping him. We had been able to benefit from a more successful working relationship with the school and our report reflected this. To give some idea of how we approached the parents' report, I have included some examples of the sort of items we covered in our report for the referral that resulted in Peter getting his statement.

What we included in our report for Peter

1. *Diagnoses*: a long list in our case!

2. *Barriers to accessing the curriculum*, such as:

    • handwriting issues

    • attention difficulties.

    Example: Peter has been able to try using an amanuensis – a scribe to write down work. He has also been able to have an adult present for some of the time in class, who is able to help him stay on task. It is clear from a classroom observation that the school is in complete agreement with us: Peter has shown that he does benefit from having adult support in class. This helps him to stay on task and to produce work that is truly his own and reflects his actual ability.

3. *Suggestions for removing barriers* to Peter accessing the curriculum:

    • laptop

    • typing tutor programme

- amanuensis (scribe to sit with him in his lessons and write for him).

Example: Peter's physiotherapy report highlights his very poor motor skills development. Dyspraxia was diagnosed by Great Ormond Street Children's Hospital last month. Also, lax ligaments in Peter's hands were, for the very first time, diagnosed by his physiotherapist. This explains his very real pain and difficulty in producing written work. Peter needs to develop his ICT skills and skill in using a scribe to enable him to access the curriculum.

4. *Difficulties in numeracy and spelling.*

5. *Autistic spectrum disorder and Peter's emotional life* at school:

- social communication difficulties

- need for adult teaching assistant to be present to facilitate social interaction and to help him communicate with others.

Example: Peter has very real difficulties with social interaction with other children. He will benefit from social skills training. His statement should specify provision for an adult to be free to both facilitate positive social interaction between Peter and his peers and to help him talk through ways of improving his social interaction skills both in the classroom and on the playground. He needs to be able to have adult support in these areas both as his difficulties occur and also at fixed times in the week so that the different aspects and themes of successful social interaction can be explored.

6. *Task avoidance and stress*:

- unnecessary trips to the toilet

- keeping staff talking so that Peter 'runs out' of time to finish a task

- hand washing – due to OCD, but also Peter knows that this is an activity that uses up lots of time.

7. *Mobility*:

- effects of multiple surgeries on mobility.

Example: Peter's participation in playground games is severely limited by his poor coordination and orthopaedic problems. He cannot catch a ball and is very often socially excluded by his physical disability because he cannot run about like other children.

8. *School absences and illness*:

- Peter had a long history of absence caused by surgeries, attending appointments, fatigue, childhood illness and stress.

Example: Peter often struggles to function at school because his frequent absences due to illness, fatigue and stress have led to him missing large parts of the curriculum. He will need adult support in class to provide a remedial curriculum and to help him overcome the effects of absence on his progress at school.

WHAT IS A STATEMENT OF SPECIAL EDUCATIONAL NEEDS AND WHAT SHOULD WE PUT IN IT?

In the *SEN Code of Practice* (DCSF 2001a), the description of the structure of the statement of special educational needs begins on p.100, in Section 8:29. It is a broad outline that all statements must follow. It is split up into six categories (see the LEA information pack) and they should all be packed with helpful strategies and resources to support your child at school. Remember Chapters 1 and 2? You should have lots of information about your child and will have built very positive relationships with the professionals involved in your child's education and health care. In other words you will have a great deal of evidence in the form of written reports with which to build your child's statement. Although the LEA owns the statement and is responsible for writing it, parents do have the right to comment on it and to object if they disagree with it. Very often parents can talk to the LEA officer involved in writing the statement to negotiate changes before it is made final.

Remember, a statement is only any good if it is well written. I was recently in the uncomfortable position of having to concede that William's statement had some weaknesses. Perhaps we got complacent as his primary school was providing well for his special educational needs by the end of his time there. However, we had to address it urgently in view of his imminent secondary school transfer. The words we use to describe our children's special needs and the provision needed to meet those needs, are terribly important. We must always name any needs, specify the provision to meet those needs, and be clear about *how much* provision our child will receive in terms of hours. For example, if a child needs speech therapy, we should have in the statement say, 40 minutes of speech therapy on a weekly basis, at school, and that the parents and teacher will be supported by the speech therapist in applying the therapy at home and in class. Words and phrases such as 'regular', 'access to', or 'frequent', without specified provision should be outlawed.

Once all of the information requested by the LEA is gathered together they will consider it and decide whether or not to issue a statement. Below is an example of a statement. If the LEA decides to give your child a statement, this is what it should look like. The headings in italics have been taken directly from this source and I have also included under each heading some examples of how statements ought to be written. I cannot reproduce my children's statements here because the LEA owns those documents and I do not have permission to use them. However, I hope to give an impression of how a statement is put together and what it should look like.

AN EXAMPLE OF A STATEMENT OF SPECIAL EDUCATIONAL NEEDS

'Part 1: Introduction: The child's name and address and date of birth. The child's home language and religion. The names and address(es) of the child's parents'

This section is for the accurate recording of all the basic facts about the child and parents, and it also lists the reports and other evidence considered by the LEA in writing the statement. These are listed in appendices of the statement.

'Part 2: Special Educational Needs (learning difficulties): Details of each and every one of the child's special educational needs as identified by the LEA during statutory assessment and of the advice received and attached as appendices to the statement'

This is the place where your child's special needs should be listed in as much detail as possible. It has to be said that some statements are very imprecise in this area, with the obvious effect of costing less to implement. It is the parent's job to ensure that as much detail as possible goes into the statement.

In this section the child's special educational needs are described. The examples below cover some areas of difficulty commonly experienced by children with ADHD, Asperger Syndrome and dyspraxia, such as:

- *Cognition and learning* – This should outline any learning issues the child has, and any disparity between the child's apparent ability and his actual achievement.

- *Communication and social interaction* – Does the child have age-appropriate social skills? Can he form friendships and get along with his peers? He may also take instructions literally and have impulsive behaviours, or inappropriately try to control his environment.

- *Fine motor difficulty* – Does the child have motor difficulties that impact on his learning and achievement and his ability to record his own school work in class? Other areas in which children with the combination of ADHD, dyspraxia and AS may experience difficulties are gross motor skills and information processing.

- *Parent and pupil views* – This area should cover any worries the child or parents may have. The parents' views will be canvassed in the statutory assessment process and the child will be asked to complete a pupil participation form in school.

'Part 3: Special Educational Provision: The special educational provision that the LEA consider necessary to meet the child's special educational needs. (a) The objectives that the special educational provision should aim to meet'

- *Cognition and learning* – The aim is for the child to develop his listening and attention skills so he can remain on task and become able to complete his school work independently.

- *Communication and social interaction* – The aim is for the child to develop his ability to understand and use appropriate, language in social and learning situations.

- *Fine motor difficulty* – The aim is for the child to learn to independently plan, deliver and comment on school work in line with his peers.

'(b) The special educational provision which the LEA considers appropriate to meet the needs set out in Part 2 and to meet the objectives'

- *Cognition and learning* – To meet such needs any child will have an individual plan to increase his attention and concentration skills. It will be set by the specialist teaching service, SENCO and class teacher. It will be supported by a teaching assistant whose involvement is likely to depend on allocated hours. Success will be reinforced by rewards.

  ° The child may be supported in his work by the use of written and visual prompts used by the TA to keep him on task. He may use a timer to help him plan work effectively. He will be encouraged to dismiss distractions and will be rewarded for doing so.

  ° The child will have a behaviour management programme to be specified by specialist teaching staff.

  ° The child is to be praised for his great ideas for work, and may be given a Dictaphone or have the TA write his work down for him.

This programme will be written in detail in an IEP using advice from an educational psychologist and specialist teaching service. It will be monitored as required, at least termly.

Communication and social interaction needs may be met by:

- *Speech and language provision* – A speech and language therapist will set up an appropriate speech and language therapy programme to be implemented both at home and at school, where it will be reinforced by the TA.

- *Fine motor difficulty* – Remedies for the fine motor difficulties include occupational therapy referrals, handwriting programmes, access to an amanuensis (a person assigned to write down the work a child dictates), and touch typing programmes. The frequency of these measures will be set in the statement. If IT interventions are specified, the equipment necessary should be provided by the LEA who will commit to providing and maintaining all equipment and software.

An actual statement can run to many pages and goes into great detail about what a child's difficulties are and what will be done about them. This is how it should be. I have simplified matters for clarity, but statements may well have many items under Parts 2 and 3. Again, the LEA will prepare the draft statement and parents can get a lot of help to consider whether it is fit for purpose from parent support organisations.

'(c) The arrangements to be made for monitoring progress in meeting those objectives, particularly for setting short-term targets for the child's progress and for reviewing his progress on a regular basis'
Monitoring would be in the form of setting up a new Individual Education Plan at the beginning of each term, seeking both parents' and the child's input into setting targets, an effective home/school liaison – we favoured a daily diary – and annual reviews which are a statutory part of this process.

'Part 4: Placement: The type and name of school where the special educational provision set out in Part 3 is to be made or the LEA's arrangements for provision to be made otherwise than in school'
Schedule 27 of the *Education Act 1996* says:

> Parents may express a preference for the maintained school … they wish their child to attend … LEAs must comply with a parental preference unless the school is unsuitable for a child's age, ability, aptitude or special educational needs or the placement would be incompatible with the efficient education of the other children with whom the child would be educated, or with the efficient use of resources. LEAs must consider parental representations and arrange any meeting(s) with LEA advisers or officers the parents seek, before issuing the final statement.

The suitable placement should depend entirely on the needs of the child. Most children benefit from a placement in a mainstream school with appropriate support written into their statements. Some children, however, may benefit from a special school or a private special school. Take advice from relevant support organisations and visit as many schools as you can think of that may meet your child's needs.

'Part 5: Non-educational needs: All relevant non-educational needs of the child as agreed between the health services, social services or other agencies and the LEA'

Part 5 outlines any non-educational needs the child may have. These may be specified by the local authority, health services, social services or other. Please note that this part of the statement is not legally binding and cannot be appealed through the tribunals system. Some LEAs put speech issues here, although it has been argued in the courts that speech therapy is actually an *educational* provision.

'Part 6: Non-Educational Provision: Details of relevant non-educational provision required to meet the non-educational needs of the child as agreed between the health services and/or social services and the LEA, including the agreed arrangements for its provision'

- Non-educational provision may relate to referrals to children's mental health services or any other medical services needed by the child, help from social services, or provision to meet transport need. Also, if a child needs to rest during the school day, the provision to accommodate this might well end up being written into this section.

- Sometimes speech therapy ends up in Parts 5 and 6. Parents who found their child's speech therapy put into these Parts, which made therapy provision unenforceable, successfully appealed in 1989. This provides a stated case that we can refer to, to ensure that speech therapy goes into Parts 2 and 3, where it is legally binding. This stated case is known as the Lancashire Judgment 1989.

'Signature and date'

This example of how a statement may be put together was written with reference to 'Writing the Statement' from the *SEN Code of Practice*, (DCSF 2001a, p.100, Section 8:29).

All the advice obtained and taken into consideration during the assessment process must be put into the appendices to the statement.

APPROVING YOUR OWN STATEMENT

Above is our example of how a proposed statement should look. Parents should read thoroughly Chapter 8 of the *SEN Code of Practice* because there is a lot of valuable information in it about statements. The education officer in the child's case will usually draft the statement, and it will be sent to the parents for approval.

At the point where you hold your child's statement in your hand, it is tempting to think 'phew, we did it!', and to collapse in a big heap, grateful that the whole thing is over. However it's not actually over yet. It is vitally important to ensure that the statement is well written if you are to get the best out of this for your child.

Guerrilla Tips

- Ensure that it meets his needs.
- You will have a specified amount of time in which to reply to the LEA and to make clear any objections or particular points you may want to make. You can also ask in writing for a meeting with the person who prepared the statement.
- Each special educational *need* should match up with special educational *provision*.
- Therapy should be quantified. For example, if speech therapy is outlined as a need the provision should be represented in terms of quantified hours.
- If any equipment such as a laptop, for example, is specified as a need in Section 3a, ensure that the statement says that one will be provided for your child's use in Section 3b.
- Read the statement thoroughly and object to any vague wording. For example if a child needs occupational therapy, and the statement says that your child will have 'access to occupational therapy' – or similar, this is not good enough. The statement should provide for a specific number of hours, for example, 'one hour a week delivered by a teaching assistant who will be trained by an OT during termly visits to school'.
- Discuss the content of the statement with the SENCO at your child's school. By now you should have some idea as to how helpful he or she is. If you are not comfortable with talking to your SENCO, ask one of the parent support organisations for help.

Remember the Guerrilla Mum Mantra: Don't take no for an answer, never give up. If in doubt, telephone, email and write letters.

Unfortunately, we can never assume that the draft statement will be comprehensive, or will even be well written. We once received a proposed statement that actually offered our son fewer hours of support than he had before we embarked upon the statutory assessment procedure. Believe it or not, this wasn't an error and we had to negotiate hard to get the number of hours increased to what he needed.

EMERGENCY PLACEMENTS

It can be necessary to make an emergency placement for a child either due to a sudden change in his medical circumstances, a serious deterioration in behaviour or where a child arriving unexpectedly in the area shows such severe difficulties that a statement is immediately thought to be the best way of meeting need. An emergency placement also kick-starts the statutory assessment procedure, a particular advantage if parents have struggled to gain the attention of the LEA and are in the position where they have new information in terms of a diagnosis or anything else that fits the criteria for requesting an emergency placement. The criteria are outlined on pp.99–100 of the *SEN Code of Practice*, in Sections 8:23 to 8:28.

Section 8:23 states:

In exceptional cases it may be necessary to make an emergency placement for a child, for example where:

(a) the child's medical circumstances have changed suddenly, causing a rapid and serious deterioration in the child's health or development.

(b) the parents, school, relevant professionals and the LEA agree that a sudden and serious deterioration in the child's behaviour make the child's current placement untenable or unsafe.

(c) where a child arriving unexpectedly in the LEA exhibits such significant learning difficulties as would normally warrant a statement the LEA should consult the parents and those immediately concerned, including the previous LEA, about the most appropriate placement.

(d) where a young person returns home from a secure unit or young offender's institution.

(DCSF 2001a)

This means that if a child's circumstances warrant it, then they can be placed in a specialist educational setting for the purposes of statutory assessment. They don't have to wait for the statutory assessment process to be completed. The lesson to be taken from this is that children receiving a new diagnosis may benefit from an emergency placement in a specialist setting if their parents are quick off the mark. The benefit is that obtaining a statement can take six months, but a statutory assessment is immediately triggered as soon as the emergency placement begins. Any reports from staff in specialist placements carry great weight. William received his diagnosis of verbal dyspraxia when he was four, around eight weeks after he started school. We immediately requested an emergency placement using the criteria contained within the *SEN Code of Practice.* By January he was able to start in a specialist speech and language placement, even though we had previously been told that there was no place available for him. His statutory assessment commenced immediately and his statement was made final that year. This was a very effective way of getting William's needs met.

Section 8:25 of the *SEN Code of Practice* (DCSF 2001a, p.100) states:

> When an emergency placement is made, the LEA should immediately initiate statutory assessment or reassessment. It is likely that the assessment will conclude that the statement should be made, or amendments made to an existing statement. If the child has been placed and will remain in a special school, a statement should always be made.

It is well worth reading around the subject of emergency placements, particularly if a diagnosis has not yet been made. Information can be found in the *SEN Code of Practice,* pp.99–100.

Guerrilla Tips

If your child's circumstances change unexpectedly they may qualify for an emergency placement in a specialist setting. Consider looking into this if:

- new medical information suddenly emerges about your child's condition
- your child moves unexpectedly from one LEA to another
- he experiences a sudden change in circumstances or a deterioration in behaviour.

MAINTENANCE: ENSURING THE SCHOOL CONTINUES TO DELIVER THE HELP YOUR STATEMENTED CHILD IS ENTITLED TO

Below are some of the ways parents can monitor and check that the provisions in the statement continue to be delivered.

Home-school diaries

We find that provision is much more likely to be delivered if the school knows that a parent is watching to see what they do. A home-school diary implies an agreement for parents and schools to communicate with each other, and is a place where parents can ask questions about their child's education. Sometimes I have an issue that can't wait but know the teacher can't always talk to me when I drop my child off at school. If I write the issue down in the diary, I know it will be seen and that I can expect a response.

Individual Education Plan meetings

Children with special educational needs should have an IEP from being on School Action. IEPs continue all the way through the Graduated Response and they are still used to set and monitor targets for children who have a statement. IEPs should be put in place to help children across the areas of communication, literacy, mathematics and behaviour. They should be written down and drawn up in partnership with the child and parents, and they should be reviewed at least twice a year. Our children's IEPs have always been reviewed three times a year which I think makes more sense and is good practice because there are three terms in a year. They should reflect short-term targets for that term and should not include more than three or four areas to work on. They should be very specific, should identify the teaching strategies to be used, and should have clear success or exit criteria.

Checking the provision in a statement continues to be delivered

Parents should talk to their children often about what they do at school. It is in this way that it may become evident if the school ceases to provide something that should be delivered under the terms of a statement.

Annual review of statement

The *SEN Code of Practice* provides for statements to be reviewed yearly but if circumstances change significantly for a child then an early review may be called. If you think your child's statement needs to be looked at early, especially if you are not certain that all the provision is being delivered, look up 'Reviews' in the *SEN Code of Practice* to see where you stand (DCSF 2001a, Chapter 9, Sections 9:1–9:69).

Guerrilla Tips

The statutory assessment process is the only way to be sure that the needs of a child with significant special educational needs will be met.

- As with medical professionals, keep records of all interactions or discussions with education officers.

- If you have a meeting or a telephone conversation, write an account of the discussion, or minute it, and send them a copy. This is essential.

- If they do not disagree with what you have written, take it as a tacit agreement that they agree with your account.

- Be ready to use these records as evidence if you go to mediation in the event of a disagreement.

- The *SEN Code of Practice* advocates that we should always try to mediate with the LEA, even if an application to the tribunals' service or other such complaint is made on behalf of a child. Have discussions by all means, but only if it is clear that you can gain ground by doing so.

- Never accept an outcome obtained through mediation if it doesn't meet your child's needs. If mediation fails and there is a remedy that involves making a complaint or an appeal and mediation has failed, don't be afraid to do this.

Remember the Guerrilla Mum Mantra: Don't take no for an answer, never give up. If in doubt, telephone, email and write letters.

WHAT HAPPENS AT AN ANNUAL REVIEW?

Annual reviews are the forum in which a variety of different views on the child's progress are integrated and in which changes can be made to statements to reflect a child's changing circumstances.

Parents, the child, the child's teacher(s), relevant professionals and the education officer must be invited to attend. We find that attendance of outside professionals and education officers can depend on how stable our children's progress has been and whether it is anticipated that a sea-change is necessary. Before the reviews, schools send out a questionnaire for parents to fill in about how they feel their child is progressing and if there are any concerns they are invited to air them. If parents want change they will have had the foresight to obtain appropriate referrals for their child and will turn up to annual reviews armed with suitable reports. Therapists currently working with the child are asked to provide up to date information about their needs in the form of a report for annual reviews but as a pro-active parent it is wise to ask for these well in advance of the review.

After the Annual Review the school will fill in a report form detailing decisions made about how to move forward with the child, and the LEA will consider whether it wishes to update the statement based on these comments. There have been times when we have wanted the LEA to amend, or make changes to, a statement after an annual review and the LEA has refused to do so – which currently they are quite within their power to do. Currently a parent has to ask for a reassessment to have a statement amended (changed) if the LEA don't want to do this. Assuming the LEA decides to amend a statement the parents will receive an amended or proposed statement. Any amendments should be based on the information shared in the annual review about the child's changing needs. Parents have 15 days from the date of the letter to tell the LEA if they approve of the amendments to the statement. If so it will be finalised. If not, you can ask for a meeting to discuss the statement with the LEA officer involved. If an agreement really cannot be reached it may well be necessary to ask for a reassessment or even to consider an approach to the First-tier Tribunal (Special Educational Needs and Disability).

As an aside the Lamb Inquiry (Lamb 2009) has recommended that there be a statutory right of appeal for parents when LEAs refuse to amend statements. This would prevent parents having to ask for reassessment if their child's statement is not amended after annual review.

At its publication in late December 2009, the main message of the Lamb Inquiry was that the statementing system needs to be more ambitious regarding the outcomes of children and young people with

SEN. Children, along with their parents and carers, need to be listened to more. The system needs a radical overhaul to ensure pupils receive the support they require in order to achieve. This should involve enhanced rights and a cultural shift in the way in which schools, LEAs and other professionals work with parents and carers, and children and young people. The report made 51 recommendations for change (see Lamb 2009).

Checklist

✳ If your child has special educational needs and has an Individual Education Plan as part of the Graduated Response, keep track of whether these measures are enough to close the attainment gap between your child and his peers.

✳ If learning difficulties and low attainment persist it is important to establish if the school can do any more to help.

✳ If it cannot, then this is the time to consider asking for a statutory assessment.

✳ Speak to the SENCO to find out what your child's school thinks about the idea of asking for a statutory assessment.

✳ Read the relevant sections in the *SEN Code of Practice* and seek advice from your child's school and relevant parent support organisations before you ask for an assessment.

✳ If your child's school is supportive it is still probably best to do the referral for statutory assessment yourself using the model letter on p.65. This way you retain control of the process and your child's school can still support you through a letter of support and the advice it submits.

✳ Once you are 'in the process' ensure that you stick to the timescales and submit everything you need to in time. If you have difficulty with this, seek advice. The education officer allocated to your case can give information about how things should be done as can parent support groups.

* If disagreements occur remember to use the LEA mediation services as a first response to solve problems. You can always escalate your response if necessary.

* Remember to take care over your parents' report, focusing on your child's current difficulties in school and the steps you think it is necessary to take to help.

* Keep records of discussion or meetings about your child.

* Remember, the Graduated Response is not a series of hoops to be jumped through before statutory assessment may be requested. If you think your child's case is severe enough to warrant immediate action, take it!

* Remember to use annual reviews to keep your child's statement relevant and to ensure it continues to meet his needs. It is a 'live' document that must change as your child does.

Chapter 4

WHEN THINGS
GO WRONG

NEGOTIATING WITH SCHOOLS AND THE LEA THROUGH ITS MEDIATION AND PARENT PARTNERSHIP SERVICES AND OTHER SOURCES OF HELP

If a child has special educational needs, whether the level of need leads to a statement being issued or not, he will need a parent to negotiate on his behalf at school. Children are at school for 12 years not including sixth form studies and parents of children with special educational needs must enter into an almost endless series of negotiations with their child's school and/or LEA if their children are to reach their potential. It really is true that the squeaky wheel gets the grease! Parents of children with special educational needs must set their own goals and decide how best to achieve them. In doing so they will at some point have their requests for support refused or turned down. This will occur whether a parent is pursuing a statement or not. When this started happening to us, we were not in the habit of arguing back, or of casting about to try to find someone who could support us, we meekly accepted things as they were which of course was no help at all to our children. There are things we can do to help get what we want and there are people who can help, and parents need to know who and what these sources of support are. Most of all, parents must not give up trying for their children.

If parents have their request for a statutory assessment turned down then this is a big deal and quite rightly they should avail themselves of their right of appeal through the tribunals service. Sometimes, however, things can be resolved quickly by knowing who can help and who to ask and there is lots of encouragement to use mediation services – even when in a complaints or tribunal situation. Even when we were in the process of asking for a statutory assessment or appealing we did not stop trying to resolve issues by talking to the LEA or school. If parents are refused something that carries a right of appeal, the LEA has to offer mediation services also and it is worth trying to see if these work even if you still do the formal appeal at the same time. The documentation I had from the tribunals service said that we should still try to resolve our differences with the LEA even though the appeal was ongoing. It is very important to try anything and everything that you can think of to get a positive outcome. You might actually save your child a lot of time too as statutory processes can be very lengthy. If you can get 'the powers that be' to decide to help your child by talking directly to them, it makes sense to try. Some forms of help did not work for us, but they might work really well for other people. Some good sources of help and support are:

- Parent Partnership Service
- teachers
- one-to-one meetings with education officers
- meeting with the head of the LEA
- county councillors
- local cabinet member for Education
- Education Operations Department, DCSF
- your local MP
- the media.

Below I list some examples of how we have attempted to negotiate with these people on our children's behalf.

Parent Partnership Service

Our LEA is quite good at publicising the Parent Partnership Service, and we had great hopes that it would be helpful to us. It is supposed to be a place where parents can get free and independent advice and support regarding special educational needs. If we had just wanted *information* it would have been fine. At the time we asked them for help, our children were in KS1 and we were trying to get the school to put in place some help for Peter. We asked a Parent Partnership officer (PPO) to come along to support us. We felt that instead of supporting us at the meeting, she spent the meeting supporting the headmistress. We felt undermined as parents. Because we considered that this meeting was unhelpful, we have never had anything to do with the Parent Partnership Service since. However, I must stress that I have heard good reports about the Parent Partnership from some parents, so don't write them off without giving it a chance first.

Teachers

Your child's class teacher, subject teacher, SENCO or other teacher can be his champion in school. They will be key figures in deciding how to deliver a modified curriculum and in devising your child's IEP. Ensure that they have any key information about your child and ask for meetings to pass on information wherever necessary. The current headmaster at our children's primary school played a big part in proceedings when the LEA finally gave in and agreed to give Peter a statement. We had already appealed to the SENDIST Tribunal but were in discussions with the school and LEA also about the refusal to issue a statement. The result was that after listening to us and talking to the headmaster of the school the LEA conceded and agreed to issue Peter's statement. I am pretty sure that without the headmaster this would have taken a lot longer to achieve. He was very committed to providing lots of opportunities for Peter to access the curriculum and he made an enormous difference to his life.

Of course, there are many different types of teachers who can help at many different levels. The many TAs that work with our children are central to their learning and to helping them to achieve more independence as learners. They are always there to listen to us too and to answer questions, and are our children's advocates in school.

Of course, there are times when we have tried discussion and have been unhappy with the outcome. This is the time to take things further.

One-to-one meetings with LEA officers

The LEA is responsible for managing statements. Whenever anything in our children's provision is changed, this usually involves a LEA process such as a resourcing panel or an annual review. I have found that I have to be very involved at all stages of the processes to ensure equipment or services are delivered. If I am not then even though provision might be agreed, nothing can happen for weeks or months. Some examples of reasons why we have had one-to-one meetings with LEA officers are outlined below.

GETTING A LAPTOP FOR WILLIAM

It was recently agreed that William would require a lightweight laptop for secondary school. We discussed this in January and the LEA only discussed it in a resourcing panel in July after much prompting from me. It has only just arrived at the end of September, again only after much prompting. It seems there are no policies or obligations in place directing LEAs to deliver equipment speedily – so I had to keep asking about it so they wouldn't forget. I know if I had just waited, we would still be waiting!

GETTING VOICE RECOGNITION SOFTWARE FOR PETER

One special needs officer failed to put to a resourcing panel a request for voice recognition software after agreement about Peter's need for it had been reached at an annual review and documentation handed over. After some discussion I was unable to get her to remedy the situation so I reluctantly asked for a meeting with her line manager. The line manager listened to me and apologised and thanked us for helping to identify the SNO's ongoing training needs and we were allocated a new SNO to work with us. If we had been unable to reach an agreement about getting the statement amended so Peter could have his voice recognition software, we would have had to have asked for a review of Peter's statement which would have taken some months to achieve.

Meeting with the head of the LEA

When Peter was finally given a statement it had fewer hours of support in it than he had had without it. This was a crazy state of affairs but nobody seemed able to do anything about it. We talked to several people, going up the chain of command until we reached the head of the LEA. We were facing another SENDIST tribunal but fortunately we were able to get him to listen to us. By the end of the meeting the head of the LEA said he would like the number of hours to be reconsidered in the next resourcing panel and hinted that we would be much happier with the outcome of this panel. By the beginning of the new school year we were told that the LEA had been able to see their way clear to increasing his support hours to 32.5 hours. We finally felt able to plan for Peter's future education.

County councillors

We have approached our county councillor for help, either to ask for advice or to make him aware of a concern. He is happy to advocate with the LEA or school on our behalf. We have also asked him for advice around issues such as disability discrimination. Parents can ask for one-to-one meetings with their county councillor or can correspond by email.

Local cabinet member for Education

Our local council is run along a cabinet system similar to that of the national government. This group of local government officials is drawn from the ruling political party in power, be it Liberal Democrat, Labour or Conservative, etc., and performs the role of 'watchdog'. The cabinet meets regularly in public and members of the public can put questions to the cabinet members whether their questions are on the agenda or not. There will be a cabinet member or equivalent for Children's Services or Education in your area and you can put questions to them. We corresponded with the cabinet member for Education and copied her in on emails and correspondence during the time we were discussing Peter's statement, and preparing for our meeting with the head of the LEA. We never met her but I am sure it did no harm to keep her informed and for the LEA to know we were keeping her posted about our case. There will be similar lead elected members in your local authorities.

Education Operations Department, DCSF

This is a branch of the Department for Children, Schools and Families. They investigate how LEAs are carrying out their duties and they will look at how an LEA is being run if a parent brings up concerns, although they won't intervene in individual cases. There is a phone number that parents can ring to discuss a problem and if it is one that they can deal with they will invite you to write to them.

Your local MP

Your local elected MP will run regular surgeries in your area. We all have the right to ask our MP to take up issues on our behalf.

We met with our MP about five years ago to talk about the school's lack of action over Peter's special educational needs. The outcome was somewhat disappointing, because we did not really understand ourselves how our son's needs ought to be met, and the MP seemed to have no idea either. His parting comment at the end of the meeting was to say that he would ring our son's headmistress to ask how she was helping our son, but that he was certain that she would 'be doing whatever was necessary' to help him and that if he needed a statement he was sure the school would take care of it. He sounded just like we had three years previously, when we knew nothing about special needs and believed that the system in place would take care of everything by itself! It was a low point... But again, plenty of MPs have interests in special educational needs and may well be willing to help, especially if you, unlike us, are armed with all the relevant knowledge yourself. It has got to be worth a try.

The media

Some people have used the media to their advantage to publicise their case. The most recent cases I can think of are those that crop up at the beginning of the school year, when children do not get a place at their catchment primary school. It is not for everyone, and you have to accept that you will get some attention, not all of it positive. This has worked for some people but should be gone into with great caution. I don't think children are able to make informed choices about appearing in the media and have no idea how this might impact on their lives in the long term so I have never considered this as a course of action.

A note in hindsight

Before moving on to talking about the First-tier Tribunal (Special Educational Needs and Disability), I would like to say that although all of the above methods of discussion and negotiation have had their benefits for us, with hindsight we would not have spent so long trying to make them work. Looking back there was such a big disparity in our expectations of the LEA and what they were willing to do that it was inevitable that we were going to end up going to Tribunal over their repeated refusals to assess Peter. If there is one thing I wish it is that we had had the courage to go forward with an appeal much sooner. He was nine before he got a statement. Although he is doing well at school now, with earlier help who knows what he might have achieved or what difficulties might have been avoided? The tribunals service sends out information to parents about the process and they even sent us a video showing what a tribunal was like. The bottom line was that we were worried about our ability to be successful in this formal legal arena and of making our child's school and the LEA angry with us. I felt intimidated by the process, but what we learnt was that if mediation or conciliation fails, parents really only have the statutory routes to go down, such as appealing to SEND or making other complaints. If, despite your best efforts to use the statutory processes to resolve your child's difficulties, his needs remain unmet, then it is possible to use the First-tier Tribunal (Special Educational Needs and Disability) to appeal decisions.

THE FIRST-TIER TRIBUNAL (SPECIAL EDUCATIONAL NEEDS AND DISABILITY)
What issues can the Tribunal deal with?

On 3 November 2008 the Special Educational Needs and Disability Tribunal through which we appealed the LEA's refusals to assess or issue a statement for Peter, ceased to be. This is because of reforms to streamline the whole tribunals system. SENDIST was brought under one umbrella along with tribunals on mental health and social care. Cases are now heard by the First-tier Tribunal (Special Educational Needs and Disability). The judges who used to adjudicate in cases for SENDIST now sit in the Health, Education and Social Care (HESC) Chamber of the First-tier Tribunal. Appeals against the panel's decisions now go to the Upper Tribunal instead of to the High Court. Parents in England who have children with special educational needs, may now appeal to the First-tier Tribunal (Special Educational Needs and Disability) if they disagree with decisions made by LEAs about their children's education and they have a right of appeal. These tribunals are independent of the government who cannot influence their decisions, and they are also not connected in any way to the LEAs.

I think it is important to establish which decisions may be appealed through the tribunal. The tribunals service has produced a booklet about how to use the service called *How to Appeal an SEN Decision: A Guide for Parents* (Tribunals Service Special Educational Needs and Disability 2010). In it, the issues parents can appeal about are outlined.

You can only appeal against a final statement. That is, a proposed statement must be finalised before you can appeal it through the First-tier Tribunal (Special Educational Needs and Disability). Page 3 of this booklet says that an appeal can be made when the LEA:

- Will not **carry out a statutory assessment** of your child's special educational needs, following a request by you or by your child's school.

- Refuses to **make a statement** of your child's special educational needs, after a statutory assessment.

- Refuses to **reassess** your child's special educational needs if the LA has not made a new assessment for at least six months, following a request by you or by your child's school.

- Decides **not to maintain (decides to cancel)** your child's statement.

- Decides **not to change the statement** after reassessing your child.

- Refuses to **change the school** named in your child's statement, if the statement is at least one year old (but you can only ask for a school that is funded by an LA). This is limited to the same type of school as the school named in the statement and it is not possible to ask us to alter Parts 2 or 3.

If the LA **has made a statement**, or has changed a previous statement, you can appeal against any or all of:

- The part which describes your child's **special educational needs (part 2)**.

- The part which sets out **the special educational provision (help) (part 3)** that the LA thinks your child should receive.

- The **school or type of school named** in part 4 of the statement.

- The LA not naming a school in part 4.

(Tribunals Service Special Educational
Needs and Disability 2010)

There are, however limitations as to what the tribunals service is able to deal with. For further information on this you can access the above publication *How to Appeal an SEN Decision: A Guide for Parents*, on the Tribunals Service website. Details are in my Useful Organisations and Web Resources section. One area of difficulty with the current system is that they are unable to deal with appeals brought by parents who are unhappy that the LEA has refused to amend their child's statement after reassessment. To remedy this, the only course of action currently available to parents is to ask the LEA to reassess their child and appeal to the tribunal if the LEA refused the reassessment, or if they were unhappy with the outcome of a reassessment. Indeed, this is one of the areas of the tribunals system that the Lamb Inquiry has stated should be reviewed to give parents an automatic right of appeal if the LEA refuses to amend a statement after annual review.

How the tribunal system works and how to get help with your tribunal

If you are serious about appealing a tribunal decision, it is really important to make sure you get all the information you will need to succeed. The contact details for the tribunal service are in my Useful Organisations and Web Resources section. It is also essential to make contact with a parents' support organisation that can help you to prepare your initial appeal to the panel or tribunal. Making contact with a parents' support group will help you to ensure that you follow all the tribunal's instructions correctly, that you send things in on time, and that you prepare an effective case. I had help from a tribunals advisor from the Independent Panel for Special Educational Advice (IPSEA), and he was able to put me on the right track and make sure we focused our energies on the right things. It is also worth talking to MPs as they may have contacts that can help also.

The First-tier Tribunal (Special Educational Needs and Disability) has recently been updated and there are some new aspects to it brought in with the aim of improving the system.

Parents can also make claims about disability discrimination through the First-tier Tribunal (Special Educational Needs and Disability) panel, which is discussed in my chapter on disability discrimination in schools.

The rest of the chapter tells our tribunal story...

OUR TRIBUNAL STORY AND HOW WE MADE TRIBUNALS WORK FOR US WITHOUT PAYING THROUGH THE NOSE

When Peter was seven we decided for a second time to ask for a statutory assessment – this was duly refused. At this point we appealed to the SENDIST tribunal for the first time. We felt that as a result our relationship with the school went from difficult to impossible overnight. The appeal came after the period in which we felt our relationship with the school had deteriorated so much that it seemed as though it had become utterly dysfunctional. It was very difficult to put personal feelings aside, but we had to do this and prepare for the case. I was lucky in that I had my husband also working on the tribunal with me, and we approached it in very different ways. I felt very emotional and aggrieved for Peter but channelled this by putting a lot of time and effort into researching what Peter's rights were and how we might succeed at tribunal. I also got some help from IPSEA, and one of their tribunal supporters guided me through the process.

The hearing was held in a local hotel and when we arrived we were invited into a conference room in which three panellists were sitting at a table. I attended with my husband and we sat opposite the panel to one side and the LEA – our son's teacher, headmistress and LEA representative sat on the other side. Both sides were given opportunities to speak and to state their cases. I was able to show what Peter's needs were, his lack of progress and his need for a statutory assessment. It was more difficult to keep my emotions under control, however and I am glad that my husband was with me. While I had focused on information gathering and the legal aspects of the case, he was more able to focus on presenting a coherent case, and on making sure our evidence stood out. Our file was a very thick one and one of the tribunal panellists expressed great surprise that a child with such obvious difficulties and who had had so much intervention from medical and educational services still had so little actual help in place at school.

We really thought we had won, and that if nothing else we had shown the school's failings in the cold light of day – which was very satisfying. Two weeks later we found that we had lost the case – but only on the basis that the school had not actually put in any resources into helping Peter. Tribunals can only intervene when it is clear that the school has exhausted its resources and can do no more to help.

Therefore, in a way we did win because the school was directed by the tribunal to immediately use its resources to support Peter in school, and this they did. They would never have put in place the support Peter had in Years 3 and 4 without going through this process. He was given a package of 20 hours support from the school's own resources. Over time it was evident that this still wasn't enough, and we asked a third time for a statutory assessment when Peter was nine and had by then received his diagnosis. This time the LEA agreed to assess him but then refused to issue a statement. By now we had no fear about appealing to the tribunal and did so. Two weeks later the LEA conceded the case and Peter received his statement. We think that the realisation that we would pursue a statement for Peter until he got one and the fact that this would ultimately be costly for the LEA pushed them into conceding. So, although it can be said that we have never actually *won* a tribunal, we have been able to use them to ultimately get what our child needed.

Guerrilla Tips

If you find yourself in a tribunal situation, here are some useful tips for getting through it.

Preparation

- Ask for help from one of the parent support organisations offering this service.
- Organise any information or reports you have about your child so that you can access them quickly.
- Talk to your witnesses beforehand so you can discuss how to present your child's case.
- Research the tribunals system yourself and learn all you can about what your child is entitled to.
- If you know of any other parents who have gone through a tribunal before, ask them to share information on what it was like and what helped them.
- Try to be as calm as you can – you will do your child a disservice if you can't keep control of your emotions, both in writing your case and at the tribunal itself.

- Try to attend the tribunal with your child's other parent. If that is not possible try to get some emotional support from a friend and practical support from a parent support organisation.

On the day of the tribunal

- Get up in plenty of time on the morning of the tribunal and eat a good breakfast – even if you don't feel hungry!
- Don't be late. Arrive a little early so you can compose yourself and get to know your surroundings.
- Arrange after school child care for your child(ren) so that if the tribunal goes on for longer than expected, you won't have to rush out to collect them.
- Be prepared in case the tribunal venue may either be very hot or very cold. Wear layers and carry a cardigan so that you can either remove or add layers as required.
- Take a pack of tissues with you – tribunals can be emotional!
- Focus on the fact that the tribunal is about your child and what is best for him and put to one side any negative feelings you may have about the LEA representatives. This will help you think clearly and to present the best case you can for your child.
- Take a photograph of your child with you and also one of their paintings or a piece of work. Pass these around the panel before discussions begin. This will make your child seem more real to them and help them to focus.
- When you receive the results of the tribunal, whether you win or lose, contact the person or organisation who has been helping you in order to discuss what the outcome has been. Even if you did not win, talking over the result with a person who is experienced in dealing with tribunals may show that all may not be lost.

On the face of it parents can have a case heard in the special needs and disability tribunal free of charge. The point at which the system falls down is when parents have to call witnesses. In theory parents are at liberty to call anyone they like, and the tribunal will even summon teachers and other professionals – send a letter to the witness telling them that they are required by law to attend. Summons are used because teachers, occupational therapists, educational psychologists and so on can feel awkward going to a tribunal to give evidence on behalf of parents and against their employers who are the LEA or health authority. If they are summoned this is supposed to take the pressure off so that the witness can say they have no choice in the matter and are forced to attend. We nominated Peter's teacher and an educational psychologist. They were understandably close to the headmistress of the school and we felt that she did not want them to help us. This created such difficulty that we had to have them summoned by the tribunal. I had wondered why parents would spend money on calling private witnesses if they already had NHS and educational professionals they could call on – and this is why! It was a truly dreadful experience for us although the panel dealt well with the witnesses we called, and the right information did come out in the discussions.

However, we felt there was too much emphasis placed on whose 'side' the witnesses were on and that the sensibilities of the teachers and other professional involved in the case became the issue rather than the needs of the child. The witnesses' conflict of interests made us feel very awkward about asking questions in the panel and then we realised why some parents are prepared to pay hundreds of pounds for a private witness. The cost of this would be prohibitive to many people. I would like to see a way of gathering evidence that does not put people on opposite sides.

The second time we went to tribunal the headmaster at school was patently supportive of our case. However, he did take me to one side to say that despite how he felt personally there would soon be a stage when he would be instructed by the LEA to take their side and that it was at this stage that our relationship might get difficult.

We should all be on the child's side. Rather than a tribunal being a question of the parents *fighting* the LEA, the tribunal should put the child at the centre of this process and the outcome of the tribunal should be the result of focusing on whatever outcome is in the child's best interests.

Checklist

When schools or LEAs refuse to provide the help our children need we have a number of routes to change this.

* Think about which teachers or education officers may be sympathetic to your requests.

* Consider how your representatives such as county councillors may help.

* Try anything and everything you can think of to get the decision changed.

* However, it is important to know when you will stop trying to negotiate or change decisions through mediation and make a formal complaint.

* Do not be afraid to appeal to the First-tier Tribunal (Special Educational Needs and Disability) to challenge a decision made by the LEA and to get the help your child needs.

Chapter 5

HOW TO COMPLAIN EFFECTIVELY

HOW CAN YOU COMPLAIN MOST EFFECTIVELY WHEN, DESPITE YOUR BEST EFFORTS, YOUR CHILD'S NEEDS ARE NOT BEING MET?

It is always most beneficial to a child if differences between parents, schools and LEAs can be resolved through the various mediation services that exist for this purpose. However, parents must only accept outcomes agreed during any mediation process if they are truly representative of what the child actually needs. If you have a difficulty that cannot be resolved through these processes, it may well be time to consider a complaint. In England and Wales there are currently a number of routes you can take, depending on the nature of your difficulty. If you live in Northern Ireland or Scotland, your routes to complaining will be different than the routes outlined below, because these only apply to England and Wales. Do seek information locally. In Wales there may well be some local policy differences too, so check!

Complaining about teachers and the management of the school
If you wish to complain about your child's school then this process generally begins with talking to the class teacher. If this does not resolve your issues then you can talk to the head teacher and ultimately the governing body – write a letter addressed to the Chair of Governors. All schools must have a complaints procedure and will give out copies on request.

Complaining to the school's governing body

Once a parent has exhausted the school's complaints procedure, they may put their complaint to the school's governing body in writing. You must explain why you are complaining and also say what you would like them to do to resolve the issue. They can either deal with the complaint based on what you send, or they may deal with your complaint by inviting you to a panel meeting during which the issue can be discussed. A decision will be sent to you in writing. If you are not happy with the outcome it is then possible to take your concerns to an outside body. For example if your complaint is about a teacher's misconduct, you can take your concerns to the General Teaching Council. It is easy to see why parents are put off doing this – it can make you unpopular and there are possible repercussions on your child to consider.

The General Teaching Council

Parents who have exhausted the school's complaints procedure may complain about serious misconduct of teachers to the General Teaching Council. Where the local education authority is also the teacher's employer, you have to exhaust their complaints procedures also. Their contact details are in my Useful Organisations and Web Resources section.

The local education authority

Complaints about any aspect of the LEA can be made to the most senior officer. Ask your LEA for a copy of its complaints procedure, possibly by telephone, email or by letter. Write to the most senior officer and outline your concerns including what you would like them to do to make things right. If your complaint is about the LEA acting unlawfully or not following the *SEN Code of Practice* it is possible to have the *monitoring officer* look into things on your behalf. A complaint to the monitoring officer has to be investigated by a senior officer from another council. They have to report any irregularities they find and the relevant committee must consider their findings. From what I can gather, the monitoring officer can't actually *make* the LEA do anything. We could have complained when the LEA and school were keeping Peter down on School Action – but it was much more effective to go down the statutory assessment route – a statement was what we were really trying to achieve.

The Information Commissioner

Parents are entitled to see their children's education record within 15 days of requesting it. School documents to which parents have access, such as the school accessibility plan or SEN policy should be supplied within 20 days. Ask in writing, schools can ask you to pay for photocopying. If access to this information is denied parents can complain to the Information Commissioner. It is also possible to make a complaint to the Information Commissioner if parents think their child's school records have not been kept up to date or are inaccurate or if the records are released to unauthorised persons. Contact details for the Information Commissioner are in my Useful Organisations and Web Resources section.

How to complain about a school to OFSTED

Ofsted is the organisation responsible for inspecting schools. Schools are inspected once every three years. Schools have to notify parents of inspections and give them the opportunity to put their views to the inspectors. Ofsted can investigate a range of complaints about the school but cannot investigate concerns about individual children. For example Ofsted can look at the achievement of pupils in the school, or the way in which the school spends its money but cannot look at the provision your child has in his statement, or any particular cases of discrimination. Contact details for Ofsted are in my Useful Organisations and Web Resources section.

Complaints about the curriculum

Complaints about modification of the National Curriculum should be first made to the head teacher, and then to the governing body if parents are not happy with the outcome. If the outcome of this is not satisfactory they may then use the LEA complaints procedure. The LEA must set up a complaints procedure for parents to make complaints about the curriculum. Examples of the kind of complaint dealt with are: modification of the National Curriculum, failing to provide religious education or collective worship, failing to provide the National Curriculum, not allowing a pupil to take/drop a subject, or charging for a subject (unlawfully – sometimes it is lawful).

Educational negligence

It is possible to bring a case to the courts for educational negligence where an education professional has a duty of care to an individual, where the standard of care was very much below what was expected of that professional and where the individual has suffered damage as a direct result with their earnings being far less than they would have been had the standard of care been high. However, although there have been some high profile cases, the damages that can be awarded by the court have been less than was hoped and the costs of bringing such a case prohibitive. Legal aid is now not usually given. Action must be taken a maximum of three years from the young person's eighteenth birthday or from when they knew about the negligence and the breach of duty and the harm caused. There is no preventative route when making this sort of claim – you can only do so once the damage has been done. The law that applies is outlined in the *Education Act 1996* Part IV, including schedules 26 and 27. See also the *SEN Education (SEN) (England) (Consolidation) Regulations 2001.*

Complaining to the Secretary of State

If parents think that the LEA or their children's maintained school is behaving unreasonably or unlawfully, they can write to the Secretary of State at the Department of Children, Schools and Families (DCSF) to complain. It is generally easier to make a complaint that the LEA or maintained school is behaving unlawfully rather than unreasonably because there is no legal definition of what 'unreasonable' is exactly. Get help from a parent support organisation or one of the organisations offering free legal advice if you decide to complain to the Secretary of State, because it is very easy to get this wrong. When we wrote to the Secretary of State about the LEA issuing a proposed statement giving Peter fewer hours of TA support than he had previously been getting, our complaint was passed on to the SEN Operations Team. All we knew was that we were angry that Peter had fewer hours of help *with* a statement than *without* a statement. We had nothing so elaborate in mind as a plan to get the Secretary of State to right wrongs. We did not consider whether there may have been any legal perspective we could have used, we didn't even say we were making a complaint against the LEA for acting unreasonably in our son's case. Therefore we did not get the result we wanted. The Secretary of State has the power to direct schools and LEAs to remedy any unlawful or unreasonable Act but you do have to ask very specifically for what you want. We wanted the Secretary of State to exercise his power to direct the LEA to take action to remedy this unreasonable act but this did not happen because the Secretary of State was not obliged to treat it as an official complaint due to the way in which we worded our letter. Clearly, this is complicated and most parents would need to talk all this through with someone used to dealing with these things. Contact details for complaining to the Secretary of State are in my Useful Organisations and Web Resources section, but do get help from a parents' advice organisation too.

The local government ombudsman

The local government ombudsman looks at complaints about councils and local authorities, including education admissions, appeal panels and injustices because of maladministration. It oversees how these bodies make their decisions. Parents may complain about the LEA to the local government ombudsman if, for example, the provision in their child's statement is not delivered despite their having asked them to put that right.

They may appeal if the LEA fails to issue a statement or to comply with deadlines in the statementing procedure or decides to cease to maintain (cancel) a statement with no good reason. They will also take action where the LEA has failed to comply with its own policies with regards to your child's case. Details of how to find your local government ombudsman are in the Useful Organisations and Web Resources section.

Judicial review

If you have exhausted the appropriate complaints procedure or if the case is very urgent, you may consider applying to the courts for a judicial review. A judicial review is how the High Court supervises the way public bodies reach their decisions, and make sure that the law was properly applied. The court will look at how the public body reached their decision and check that it is lawful. If they are not happy with how the public body has exercised their power they can ask them to take the decision again.

If a judicial review is sought in relation to a matter concerning special educational needs, the person seeking the review must prove that the LEA does not have the power to take the action or make the decision it did, and must also be able to prove that the LEA was under a legal duty to act or make a decision in a particular way and has not done so. You will need legal assistance to do this. Before seeking a judicial review it may be worth complaining to the local education authority monitoring officer.

THE ISSUES AROUND MAKING COMPLAINTS

The above suggestions are starting points so that parents know where they can turn to in order to discuss the relative merits of complaining. Making a complaint is a difficult step to take and it is *vital* that parents get specialist help from one of the parent support organisations or other public bodies I have referred to if going down this route. Sometimes you need to write your letter in a specific way (as with asking for a statutory assessment), or quote relevant legislation, and if you don't express yourself in the right way or provide the right information your complaint may well fail. There are also advantages and disadvantages associated with each of these actions and you really need help to think through how complaining may help or otherwise affect your child.

Checklist

* If something happens that makes you want to complain, do all you can to remain calm.

* Decide whether you can achieve your aims through talking things through or using any mediation services that may be available.

* If this is not possible and you want to make a formal complaint, consider making contact with a parents' support organisation. They will have a lot of experience in helping people to decide how to move forward with similar issues.

* Act quickly in getting advice – speed can be very important.

* Once you have decided to complain, ensure you get good advice so that you follow the process properly.

* If a course of action requires you to consult a lawyer, approach organisations such as the Children's Legal Centre or parent support groups to see if it is possible to access free legal representation.

* Keep accurate records of all correspondence – including written records of telephone conversations.

* Get help to consider how making a complaint will improve your situation. Also consider carefully any drawbacks.

Chapter 6

HOW TO ENSURE YOUR CHILD IS HAPPY AND SAFE AT SCHOOL, AND DEAL WITH BULLYING

HOW TO HELP CHILDREN BUILD POSITIVE RELATIONSHIPS AT SCHOOL

When children start school at the age of four or five parents have a big part to play in helping them to develop good social relationships with their peers. We all need good social relationships to feel part of the world and if we feel excluded it can lead to our developing poor self-esteem and poor social relationships. The obvious route to developing friendships is through arranging play dates with, or inviting home the children your child gets on with or with whom they share an interest. Even if your child knows few children to begin with, parents can widen their social circle through meeting other parents at the school gate or when picking up their children after activities. Children can develop their interests and social relationships through joining in school activities such as lunch-time clubs, after school clubs, sports, and music and drama groups.

Children with disabilities however, often need a bit of an extra hand with social skills and building relationships. The simple play date can be very unstructured and prone to failure with one or the other child becoming bored. This kind of play date is unlikely to be repeated, and an opportunity to build a friendship can be lost. It is almost not worth doing a play date if you don't have a plan to prevent it falling flat. So have a plan. Organise your time by having a clear start and finish time that is not too long for your child to cope with.

Organise your play space. Decide what your child and the friend will do, have all the things you will need ready, and don't forget to feed them! Hungry children are grumpy children.

New government initiatives have resulted in schools offering a wider range of after school clubs based on sporting, arts and music activities. They have been invaluable in helping my children make friends. This is because they can offer a highly structured environment in which to interact and schools ensure that those running them are able to include children of all abilities. All schools are required to have a disability equality scheme under the Disability Equality Duty under the *Disability Discrimination Act 1995*, as amended in 2005. This must include strategies to ensure that children can access all the activities of the school and after school clubs are a part of this. Look at the policies at your child's school to see what they have to say on the subject.

We encouraged our children to choose spare time activities that are based on their strengths and interests and have a rule that once committed to a group, they have to try it a few times before they can decide that they don't like it. There was some initial resistance to this but now my children expect to have to stick at an activity. This enables them to give everything a fair chance and to get used to new environments. Through this approach they have formed some successful relationships.

If you are not sure how your child is doing at school socially and who their friends are, you can keep tabs on how they are doing by getting involved at school, perhaps by helping in class, being available to chaperone on school trips, or joining the Parent–Teacher Association (PTA).

Schools can improve inclusion by:

- having good playtime supervision that focuses on bullying hot spots in the playground

- increasing supervision where necessary or declaring hidden areas out of bounds

- introducing lunch-time clubs so that children who need it can elect to be indoors in a supervised setting during unstructured times, away from the noise and unpredictability of the playground

- providing lots of opportunities at break and lunch-times to engage in structured play and organised games so that children who struggle with unstructured time feel they know what to do

- organising music and drama workshops – these are popular with children and young people with a range of abilities and offer opportunities to work collaboratively and to strengthen relationships. This can also be used as an opportunity to develop songs and plays against violence and bullying

- establishing playground play schemes based on a series of set activities that anyone can join in so that nobody has to feel they have no-one to play with

- setting up mentoring systems – this is where a child with strong social skills provides support to a child with social communication difficulties by being their 'buddy' in school.

These initiatives do not have to cost a lot of money and they can make a huge difference to the lives of children with special educational needs.

BULLYING AND CHILDREN WITH SPECIAL EDUCATIONAL NEEDS OR DISABILITIES

It is now widely accepted that children with special educational needs or disabilities are more likely to be bullied at school. Up until recently, it was common for bullying to be seen as a rite of passage that most children would inevitably go through during childhood. All bullying is unacceptable. It is very damaging to a child's self-esteem and achievement at school and its impact on future life chances is enormous. It is imperative that when bullying happens in schools it is taken seriously and is dealt with effectively, and that the victim is cared for.

Children with disabilities are doubly vulnerable because they may not realise that what they are experiencing is bullying. If they have social communication difficulties they may also not be able to communicate effectively to tell someone that they are being bullied. When a bullying situation first develops it is not unusual for the bully to claim that it is 'a joke', and that physical bullying is 'just play fighting'. Both behaviours are actually very upsetting and inflicting real pain but if they are done smilingly and in the context of a game, the victim may feel unable to object. With this in mind it is wise to be on the look-out for signs of bullying and to gently investigate when signs are observed. Signs we have seen in our own children are:

- unexplained cuts, bruises or injuries

- lost or stolen clothes or personal objects

- our child being sad or depressed or showing a sudden change in behaviour

- our child crying but unable to say why

- our child becoming very tired – not being able to sleep, or trying not to go to sleep at bedtime to make the morning come slower!

Other signs could be:

- your child is starving after school because lunch money has been taken away

- your child takes a long time to get to and from school in a bid to avoid bullies who might be encountered on the way

- your child becomes withdrawn

- a decline in the quality of school work

- self harm!

The different types of bullying can be:

- verbal bullying – insults and taunts

- excluding from play – suddenly child is not allowed to play and other children are told not to play with victim

- physical bullying – injuries, pushing, chasing, kicking, scratching, either by an individual or by a group

- bystanders who do not report the bullying to a teacher collude in the bullying by allowing it to continue to happen unchecked

- cyber bullying – abusive comments via the internet or mobile phones

- racial bullying – physical harm, verbal, emotional or cyber bullying on the basis of race or colour.

Children with special educational needs may attract a number of bullies and bullying behaviour. Generally boys have tended to be more involved in physical bullying although they can, like girls tend to do, exclude, ridicule and taunt. Children with disabilities, particularly those on the autistic spectrum can find it very difficult to regulate their responses and become more likely to be bullied because of their very 'entertaining' reactions.

Schools are not only obliged to prevent and to deal with bullying, they also have to take into account the special issues around disability bullying. I wish I had known this when my children were small, it would have saved me a lot of trouble because I would have known what to demand of their school, as outlined below.

DISABILITY BULLYING: WHAT CAN WE EXPECT SCHOOLS TO DO ABOUT IT?

Safe to Learn is a relatively recent government strategy that aims to make the prevention of bullying a priority in all our schools. There are many *Safe to Learn* and other government anti-bullying strategy documents available to view on the Teachernet website. They make interesting reading. However, the *Disability Discrimination Act 2005* makes a distinction between the bullying that happens to children without disabilities and the bullying that happens to children with disabilities. It establishes a duty for local education authorities to take further steps than those laid down under the *School Standards and Framework Act 1998* and to make it a priority to tackle disability bullying in schools.

Preventative work

Preventative work will include implementing whole-school programmes such as through the PSHCE (personal, social, health and citizenship education) curriculum that offers specific opportunities to discuss bullying and the *Safe to Learn* or Social and Emotional Aspects of Learning programmes (SEAL). *Safe to Learn* clearly sets out the school's obligations to keep records of all bullying relating to children who have disabilities or special educational needs. This enables schools to see if their strategies are being effective and if they are not, to work more effectively towards meeting their specific duty under the *Disability Discrimination Act* to eliminate disability related harassment. The SEAL programme is a whole-school programme and works on improving the emotional literacy of children. More information on these programmes can be found by following the links in my Useful Organisations and Web Resources section. Any whole-school programme should be evaluated regularly by consulting the whole school community taking into account the views of children with a range of abilities. They must reinforce the anti-bullying message through using resources like:

- posters

- anti-bullying songs

- drama workshops about disability, difference and bullying

- presentations

- children doing online research about bullying to find out information for their school

- assemblies with a focus on difference.

Mainstream schools may well have preventative measures in place but we need to ensure as far as we can, and preferably before deciding which school our child will attend, that a school is meeting its obligations under the *Disability Discrimination Act* and does not simply have a 'one size fits all' series of measures in which the particular problems of children with disabilities or special educational needs are not considered. In establishing preventative programmes or responding to bullying, schools should be able to demonstrate an ability to consider the strengths and weaknesses of the children involved. For example, children with language difficulties are less likely to be able to identify verbal bullying and they may be less able to use verbal 'fogging' techniques (described in the Guerrilla Tips box on p.116) to protect themselves. Children with emotional and behavioural problems may struggle to understand that certain behaviours of their own and others may be construed as bullying. Children with autism may know they are upset but may find it difficult to pinpoint how exactly they have been bullied. Some children may struggle to recall events if bullying episodes are not followed up quickly, but similarly other children may need time to process a sequence of events before they can have a meaningful discussion about what happened.

Responsive work

Responsive work is carried out through dealing effectively with bullying incidents as they occur and through devising and implementing the school's anti-bullying policy. A school's response to bullying should reflect the need to:

- ensure children can trust that they will be listened to if they report bullying and that effective action will be taken

- recognise that a number of children with SEN or disabilities may either not recognise they are being bullied, may be unable to report that they are being bullied or may be afraid to tell

- use creative ways of reporting bullying, for example by using questionnaires, bullying boxes, or nominating particular staff to help and to communicate with children.

To ensure children feel confident they can report bullying and be heard, schools should:

- look out for changes in a child's behaviour that can indicate a bullying issue

- provide a quiet place in which to talk

- consider the child's communication needs – do they have the right tools?

- ensure children can understand the person (member of staff) speaking to them about the bullying

- ensure children have had enough time to calm down and have been able to express fully what they want to say

- allow children plenty of time to talk

- check the understanding of children with disabilities, for example children with autism are often assumed to comprehend much more than they actually do

- use prearranged signals that children can use to indicate they have been bullied and need to talk, without drawing undue attention to themselves

- ensure a teacher will check on a bullied child several times a day or week or as necessary to find out if things are going well or not

- initially treat *all* reports of bullying as being truthful – children must know they will be believed if they report bullying because they often think they will be disbelieved if they report it

- be aware that children with disabilities or special educational needs are more at risk of bullying

- communicate well across the school about specific children where bullying is an issue

- be aware if a child has emotional or behavioural issues that make him more likely to be a bully, so they can help the child change their behaviour if necessary.

The overall aim must be to enable the child to have confidence that he will be understood and that action will be taken.

WHAT TO DO WHEN YOUR CHILD IS BULLIED: HOW CAN YOU HELP YOUR CHILD COPE?

If your child is bullied, especially if the bullying takes the form of hitting or other physical bullying, it is not helpful to demand that your child hits the bully. For many children physical violence is just not in their nature and it can simply increase pressure and give them the idea that they are failing you if they cannot respond in this way. It can also result in further injury or put the child in more danger.

When a child reports bullying to a parent, the first thing to do is to stay calm. This can be very difficult, especially if the child has been bullied before. Praise them for being brave enough to tell you about the bullying and tell them that they are not to blame for it. Reassure your child that there is nothing wrong with him, he is fine. Explain that the bully has chosen him as a target because he has his own problems and has decided to vent that sadness or anger on someone else. If your child has been badly hurt or is severely distressed you may need to seek medical advice. Explain to your child that the bully has probably chosen to bully him because he imagines that he can get away with it. Bullies don't like their bullying to be too difficult and they expect certain behaviour from their victims. They do it for status and to appear tough to their peers. If your child stops responding in the expected way, the bully will probably give up and lose interest. Even if your child is traumatised or scared there are some things you can suggest that he does, which I outline in the Guerrilla Tips box below.

Guerrilla Tips

If your child is being bullied, here are some things that you and your child can do to help the situation.

- If the bullying is physical, tell your child not to fight back – this can prolong the bullying and put your child at risk of harm.
- Ask your child to nominate a couple of people he thinks he could talk to at school if there is a problem with bullies at school. Ensure the people nominated are aware of the situation and easily accessible to your child at playtimes when bullying is likely to happen.
- Suggest that he avoid the bully by playing a different game in a different place.
- Perhaps your child can think about making new friends at school.
- If verbal bullying occurs, your child could say loudly 'Can you please repeat that so the teacher can hear?' The bully won't be expecting this and may well move on.
- Your child could be a broken record – if he is bullied, he could repeatedly say 'I don't like that, it's bullying', until the bully gives up.
- Your child could agree with the bully so that there is no reason to go on about something. For example, 'You've got glasses, you're speccy' – 'Yes I know'.
- Fogging – this is a tactic against verbal bullying in which the target imagines himself to be in a big bubble or cloud and protected from the comments. Nothing can get through to him. The bully gets no response and gives up.

- Walk tall – children who exhibit positive body language and look confident, as if they know where they are going and what they are doing, are less likely to be bullied.

- Encourage your child to take up some free time activities outside of school where they can pursue an interest and meet new people to be friends with. Success in this will improve their confidence at school.

- Find out from the school about buddy schemes etc. It may be that your child can have a buddy to help with moving from class to class, during unstructured time and also someone to walk to and from school with.

- Remember to take into account your child's abilities and difficulties before deciding what you will suggest. The aim is to make bullying unrewarding so that the bully will desist, rather than retaliate.

Some anti-bullying organisations offer assertiveness training for children. These courses are designed to empower children so that they become less likely to be the target of bullies. Contact anti-bullying agencies to ask if they are providing such courses. Self defence classes can improve confidence and help a child to learn not to appear as a victim. We have found it helpful to have some targets relating to assertiveness and social skills written into our children's Individual Education Plans and have helped them to get as involved and as invested as possible in school activities so that they feel they are a valued part of the school. They have also been part of the KS1 playground friends' scheme acting as mentors to younger children. When bullying arose, we also attended meetings with teachers to discuss the problems in depth. Before deciding to take this step it is important to have a strategy so your emotions don't take control of the meeting.

Cases of bullying at school will normally be dealt with by the school. However, if there has been a more serious assault or theft then you should consider reporting it to the police. Even if the bully is under the age of criminal responsibility the incident should be recorded as a crime. Also, bullying on the basis of disability, ethnicity or sexuality should be recorded by the police as a hate crime. If the school is being cooperative and helpful, discuss this course of action with them first, as they may prefer alternative solutions at least initially.

Guerrilla Tips

Consider the points below when deciding to go into school to discuss bullying.

- Try to be calm, it sounds easy but can be very difficult.
- Make a list of questions to ask and points to make before the meeting and take it with you.
- Talk to your child's teacher about what has happened and ask him or her what they have observed.
- Ask teachers what they are doing to resolve the situation.
- Ask to see a copy of the anti-bullying policy and find out how the school will deal with bullying and how they are applying the policy to your child's situation.
- Ask the school to keep a log of all bullying incidents and also to record how each incident is dealt with. If a log has already been started ask to see it at each meeting.
- Ask the school to keep the bully separate from your child as far as possible until the situation is resolved.
- Find out what sanctions (if any) are being applied to the bully as a deterrent.
- Fix a date, perhaps in a week, to go back and discuss progress – has the bullying stopped?
- Keep your requests reasonable – for example, the school is unlikely to expel a bully no matter how much we might wish it.
- If you are unhappy with the class teacher's response, ask to see the head teacher of the school to discuss how to proceed.
- If you are not happy with the head teacher's response, or if the bullying does not stop, write a letter to the Chair of Governors asking them to deal with the situation.
- Take notes of all meetings with teachers and record what action has been agreed about the bullying.
- If there is still no improvement you are entitled to make a complaint to the LEA.
- Be really careful if you decide to confront the bully's parents directly. To do this you need to be really sure of a reasonable reception and that you will be able to communicate effectively with them.

> 🐾 **Alongside these measures remember to do all you can to work on your child's self-esteem through providing lots of opportunities for them to enjoy doing the things they are good at.**
>
> 🐾 If your child's work is suffering, or the bullying is causing chronic anxiety or health issues then this is the point at which parents should start to consider seriously a move to another school.
>
> *Remember the Guerrilla Mum Mantra: Don't take no for an answer, never give up. If in doubt, telephone, email and write letters.*

In addition to carrying out these strategies above we have also made a point of nurturing our children's interests outside of school so they can develop friendships elsewhere and a sense of self-belief. These are especially important when school is not going so well. William enjoys playing rugby and this is an area where his talent for running into things and people is actually celebrated! Both of our children are musical and derive a lot of self-confidence from playing instruments and taking part in school shows. These things are a source of pride to the children and help with self-confidence. There is nothing better for your child than being successful at an activity they love doing. Find concrete ways for your children to experience success. It is one thing to tell our children how great they are but they will only really develop self-belief when they experience success for themselves. This will help to protect them from the effects of bullying.

DIFFERENT TYPES OF ANTI-BULLYING POLICIES: HOW TO TELL IF YOUR CHILD'S SCHOOL HAS A GOOD ONE – OR NOT!

Before I had to help my children to deal with bullying I believed that if it happened the school would be able to deal with it effectively. I don't know why I thought that, it was one of those things to which I had never given much thought and took for granted. I never imagined it would ever be a problem that could not be solved. Perhaps I thought that teachers received special training in their teacher training courses, or that the government had a strategy in place that schools had to adopt. My understanding of how schools were supposed to deal with the problem was hazy and this was very much to my children's detriment. The fact is that although schools do have to develop an anti-bullying policy, they decide for themselves what *sort* of policy it will be.

In recent years there has been some discussion about the relative merits of a variety of different approaches to bullying and anti-bullying policies and this has led to schools adopting a range of different types of approaches when writing their policies. It is important to understand the school's approach because this will completely inform the content of the policy and the actions the school is able to take when bullying occurs. Some common approaches are described below.

Circle time or circle of friends

A lot of primary schools use this approach. Children sit on the carpet in a circle and after engaging in a play activity any issues needing discussion – including bullying – may be brought up in a group discussion. One of the main aims of this process is to develop a safe place for discussing the feelings and needs of other people, where members listen actively to each other and value difference. The drawback with this is that the child has to talk about these hurtful experiences in front of the whole class and children often feel too embarrassed to do this. Some bullies are quite gratified to hear about the results of their bullying in circle time. My children's primary school does circle time and I have never known it to improve a bullying situation or to prevent bullying from recurring.

The no-blame approach

The 'no-blame approach' does not seek to apportion blame or to punish a bully. If a bullying incident occurs, then the victim is spoken to by a teacher who does not ask *what* happened, but seeks to establish the victim's feelings, and which children were involved or present. A group of children not including the victim, but including the bully, the victim's friends, children who are not particularly friendly with the victim and any bystanders present, is asked to meet and the incident is discussed. The teacher may read out a piece of writing done by the victim, another piece of writing or a piece of poetry to highlight the effects of the bullying. No blame is apportioned but the group is given responsibility to help the child. About a week later the group meets to discuss progress. The theory is that the group has taken on responsibility for improving matters for the bullied child and that the bullying is eradicated. This approach has a number of disadvantages in my experience. At the group discussion stage when the victim is absent, the bully may well use this opportunity to misrepresent events. This might go unchallenged if the group is not confident enough to speak up. Also, the victim is encouraged to write about their innermost feelings and is made much more vulnerable because the bullies learn how effective their tactics have been and can use the information gained for further bullying. My children's primary also uses this approach and I can say from personal experience that it really does feel like the school is failing to act with the victim left feeling embarrassed and let down. I have not yet known this approach to stop bullying. Its nastiness simply intensifies because with each passing incident, the bullies know even better which buttons to push. Every time we brought up a bullying incident, and the school dealt with it in this way, we were indirectly handing more ammunition to the bullies.

Restorative Justice

Restorative Justice originated in New Zealand where it was used in traditional Maori healing. It has recently been brought to Britain where it is used extensively in the Youth Justice system. The victim and the offender are brought together in a safe environment where the victim has the opportunity to explain the consequences of the offender's actions. However it does not work in all cases. Some bullies show no regret whatsoever and in this scenario there is little likelihood of a successful resolution.

The bystander approach

This is a very useful approach but must be used in conjunction with good whole-school preventative work around bullying, a very strong behaviour policy and a strong anti-bullying policy. Many schools are now subscribing to the idea of being a 'telling school' and have lots of posters up declaring this to remind pupils that it is their duty as a pupil of the school to report all bullying behaviour that they may witness. The distinction is made between reporting incidents and telling tales. This is a good scheme if used together with peer mentoring schemes because bullies are swayed by peer pressure. They don't like to meet opposition to their behaviour and if they have a number of people objecting to it then they are much more likely to give up at an early stage. It also has the added advantage that incidents will be reported even if the victim is too afraid to do so themselves.

Peer mentoring schemes

This is where certain children are chosen to be trained as peer mentors to care for younger children in the school who have been bullied. They can be very effective at preventing bullying and improving social skills and confidence in the victim. They fit in well with whole-school approaches to prevent bullying and support children who have been bullied. They do involve a lot of work requiring a lot of teacher input both with the wider school and with the individual children chosen to be peer mentors. This is because the peer mentors must be well trained and supported by teachers if the volunteers are to know how to deal with the issues that will be brought to them. Of course, when new peer mentors join the course, teachers will have to repeat the training courses.

What happens is that older children are trained over some months about how to support children in the school who have been bullied. They wear special badges so that they can be easily identified as sources of help to deal with bullying. The school may also set up quiet areas or clubs to serve as havens so that children who struggle with unstructured time or who may not have friends can have things to do during breaks and somewhere to go where they will feel safe.

Straightforward punitive approach

All children in the school are made aware of the standards of behaviour expected from all pupils. The behaviour policy is enforced by teachers each and every time the rules are not followed and all pupils who break the rules are subject to sanctions and consequences for their behaviour on a continuum up to and including permanent exclusion. I firmly believe that with persistent bullies this is the only approach that works.

The Teachernet website actually offers to schools a sample anti-bullying document and recommends that schools base their policies on it. I particularly like what it has to offer in terms of practical steps to take.

Teachernet sample Anti-bullying policy

The following is intended as a model outline policy that schools can use as a starting point when devising or revising their own policy.

The aim of the anti-bullying policy is to ensure that pupils learn in a supportive, caring and safe environment without fear of being bullied. Bullying is anti-social behaviour and affects everyone; it is unacceptable and will not be tolerated. Only when all issues of bullying are addressed will pupils be able to fully benefit from the opportunities available at schools.

Bullying is defined as deliberately hurtful behaviour, repeated over a period of time, where it is difficult for those being bullied to defend themselves. The three main types of bullying are:

- physical (hitting, kicking, theft)

- verbal (name calling, racist remarks)

- indirect (spreading rumours, excluding someone from social groups).

Pupils who are being bullied may show changes in behaviour, such as becoming shy and nervous, feigning illness, taking unusual absences or clinging to adults. There may be evidence of changes in work patterns, lacking concentration or truanting from school. Pupils must be encouraged to report bullying in schools.

Schools' teaching and ancillary staff must be alert to the signs of bullying and act promptly and firmly against it in accordance with school policy.

STATUTORY DUTY OF SCHOOLS

Head teachers have a legal duty under the *School Standards and Framework Act 1998* to draw up procedures to prevent bullying among pupils and to bring these procedures to the attention of staff, parents and pupils.

IMPLEMENTATION
Schools

The following steps may be taken when dealing with incidents:

- if bullying is suspected or reported, the incident will be dealt with immediately by the member of staff who has been approached

- a clear account of the incident will be recorded and given to the head teacher

- the head teacher will interview all concerned and will record the incident

- form tutors will be kept informed and if it persists the form tutor will advise the appropriate subject teachers

- parents will be kept informed

- punitive measures will be used as appropriate and in consultation will all parties concerned.

Pupils

Pupils who have been bullied will be supported by:

- offering an immediate opportunity to discuss the experience with a form tutor or member of staff of their choice

- reassuring the pupil

- offering continuous support

- restoring self-esteem and confidence.

Pupils who have bullied will be helped by:

- discussing what happened

- discovering why the pupil became involved

- establishing the wrong doing and need to change

- informing parents or guardians to help change the attitude of the pupil.

The following disciplinary steps can be taken:

- official warnings to cease offending

- detention

- exclusion from certain areas of school premises

- minor fixed-term exclusion

- major fixed-term exclusion

- permanent exclusion.

Within the curriculum the school will raise the awareness of the nature of bullying through inclusion in PSHE, form tutorial time, assemblies and subject areas, as appropriate, in an attempt to eradicate such behaviour. The school will review this policy annually and assess its implementation and effectiveness. The policy will be promoted and implemented throughout the school.

(Department for Children, Schools and Families, Teachernet 2010)

OUR EXPERIENCE OF SCHOOL BULLYING POLICIES

This sort of policy, based on more punitive approaches, is not without its critics based on the requirement to apply sanctions. Its detractors say that punishment is not the answer and that the bullies must be engaged by making them want to change because it is the right thing to do, not because they fear punishment. My own view is that some bullies have no motivation to change and will only do so if sanctions are imposed.

To date there has been no definitive agreement about which kind of policy is the most effective against bullying. All parents will have to look at the policy at their child's school and decide whether it works based on how the school acts to deal with bullying. Our children's primary school which has just 200 children on the roll subscribes to a no-blame anti-bullying policy with elements of circle time and peer mentoring. Bullying was a recurrent theme over some years. Indeed, at times it has appeared to us that the bullies had more rights than our children!

Our children now attend a large secondary school which has an anti-bullying policy more like the Teachernet policy above. It can be construed to be a more 'punitive' approach. During the past two years that Peter has attended the school, I can count the bullying incidents involving our children on one hand and they have all been dealt with quickly and effectively. They have not recurred and Peter has been able to move on from feeling like a victim. An added benefit at this school that I believe to be a key factor in their success at dealing with bullying is their behaviour policy. It is very clear about the behaviour it requires of pupils, and is equally clear about sanctions for misbehaviour – and they follow through. Each time a child misbehaves they know that a consequence will inevitably follow. Result – a calm, orderly and industrious environment in which my son is thriving. In addition to this, Peter is also learning to cope better if bullying does happen and is not so crushed by the experience. He trusts that the school will deal with it and he feels like someone who was simply unfortunate enough to be picked on but knows how to get it resolved and to move on from the experience.

William has had a term at this school. He arrived at the school with very low self-confidence, having been bullied at primary school because he appeared different owing to his special educational needs.

He was unwilling to avail himself of much of the help that was provided for under the terms of his statement because he did not want to do anything that would make him look different. He feared that if the other children thought he was different they would not be his friend and would bully him. There have been a couple of incidents which were swiftly dealt with and he is learning to trust that his new school will deal effectively with bullying. He has started to enjoy school more and to attend a couple of after school clubs.

If, given what I know now, I had to pick a school again for my vulnerable four-year-olds I would scour the town until I found one with a very strong behaviour policy, an effective anti-bullying policy and a very strong anti-bullying ethos and very evident preventative work. Hindsight is 20/20, I know, and I also know that in many areas school choice has been severely curtailed in recent years – but this is one reason why we pursued our children's statements! The *Education Act 1996* allows parents to express a preference for a school for a child with a statement and the LEAs must (subject to certain limitations outlined in Schedule 27, *Education Act 1996*) comply with the parents' preference. If we had not had this opportunity our children would be at their catchment school which does not deal well with bullying.

WHAT TO DO IF YOU ARE UNHAPPY WITH THE SCHOOL'S RESPONSE TO BULLYING OR THE ANTI-BULLYING POLICY AT YOUR CHILD'S SCHOOL

As with any problem at school the first step to take is to try to discuss it with your child's teacher, SENCO or head teacher. This is what we did but we made the mistake of talking for far too long, and we did not understand why the bullying did not stop when the school seemed to be doing all of the right things. The school certainly did not tell us that its policy was based on the 'no-blame approach' and it did not ask us if we thought this approach was working. If it had we would have acted sooner, but like thousands of other parents we believed that the school was doing all of the right things. It will come as no surprise to hear that we got to the point where we were willing to change our children's school. William was very strongly against moving schools. He was of the view that the school was *his school* and that nobody was going to make him leave. Peter just wanted to stay where things were familiar. As they did have the benefit of having a lot of adult support written into their statements, and their time at the school was coming to a natural end, I agreed not to move them. As with many bullying situations the bullying waxed and waned and the situation was not always a desperate one. Parents can make a complaint to the Chair of the Board of Governors, if they have tried to discuss matters with their child's teachers. If you want to do this, obtain a copy of the school's complaints policy and follow it.

I finally wrote a letter of complaint to the school when William was in his final half of Year 6 and the bullying had intensified. I demanded that they protect him so that he could enjoy his final few months at the school and pointed out the school's obligations under the *Disability Discrimination Act* to deal with disability bullying. Whereas all of my other approaches over the time my children had been at the school had failed to have any effect, quoting the law to them did the trick and my complaint was upheld. For those final few months I was gratified to see, on several occasions, William's bully sitting outside the head teacher's office serving out his in-school exclusions. It still looked like the easy option to me but it was something and it meant a lot to William to see that they were finally doing something about the bullying. They are also going to review their policy. It is too late for William, but may at least help other children if they change it.

THE EFFECTS OF BULLYING

We have all seen the newspaper articles detailing children driven to depression or desperate measures of self harm or suicide when schools fail to address the problem of bullying. Many schools have active anti-bullying policies that are based on ineffective approaches. Until more schools commit themselves to ensuring that they are safe places, and to dealing effectively with bullying by adopting effective methods of dealing with the problem I can't see this situation changing.

My children have been emotionally scarred by their experiences of being bullied in primary school. Years of bullying have led to their having high levels of anxiety, low self-esteem, low self-confidence and feelings of low self-worth. Both were underachieving when they transferred to secondary school. Thanks to their new school's firm approach to bullying this is now slowly changing with them both achieving a certain amount of social and academic success. Their experience of school has been transformed.

OBTAINING FREE AND OBJECTIVE ADVICE ABOUT BULLYING

There are several support organisations such as Bullying UK and Kidscape who will give free advice to parents dealing with a bullying situation. Contact details are in my Useful Organisations and Web Resources section. If your child's school is not taking disability bullying seriously this can be a discrimination issue as the *Disability Discrimination Act* states that schools must make it a priority to tackle this issue. Further advice on this issue can be obtained from the Equality and Human Rights Commission – contact details also in the Useful Organisations and Web Resources section.

Checklist

* Try to do all you can to promote positive relationships for your child at school.

* Find out how your child's school promotes inclusion through preventative work, mentoring schemes, lunch-time play schemes and after school activities.

* Find out if your child's school has made it a priority to deal with disability bullying.

* If your child is bullied reassure him and try to give him strategies for dealing with it.

* Do not try to deal with the bully yourself – leave this to the school.

* It is best to let your child's school talk to the bully's parents. However, schools do not always involve the bully's parents in discussions. If you do decide to approach parents yourself, take great care as this can backfire.

* Ask for a copy of the school's anti-bullying policy and behaviour policy.

✳ Ask your child's school to keep records of all incidents and also to record how they deal with them.

✳ If the bullying is persistent discuss with the school what it intends to do to prevent further incidents.

✳ Monitor how your child copes with the situation.

✳ If you are unhappy with the school's response, be prepared to consider making a complaint if the bullying does not stop.

✳ Obtain all the advice you can find through the organisations in my resources section and anything else you can find. Research online to find out what can help.

✳ If your child needs it, try to access some counselling for them through your GP or through the anti-bullying support organisations.

✳ If your child's health or achievement at school is compromised because of the bullying, be ready to consider a change of schools as a last resort.

Chapter 7

SUPPORT FOR CARERS

BEING A CARER

The job of looking after a child with special needs is about so much more than just being a parent. I say this with no wish at all to minimise the job non-caring parents do. In my view though, the job of looking after a disabled child or one with special educational needs is one of the most underrated and undervalued roles that I have ever done or come across. It is also the hardest job I have ever had.

Not only do the general public not seem to notice the value of what we do, but we ourselves are guilty of it, never taking the time to pat ourselves on the back, find a way to have a break, or to find help to enable us to do our job. I think it is because the people we care for are our children. We expect to care for our children, but when your child has special needs, you have to acknowledge you have a very special role. Most other children will depend less and less on their parents as they grow up, but as children with special needs grow up they remain dependent for a lot longer. Some disabled children will never achieve independence.

It is reasonable to expect to receive help to do this very demanding role. We don't really get paid for it. A benefit is available to carers but it is a paltry sum when you consider what we could be earning if we had continued with our careers. We are on call all the time and can never 'go home' from work, because we *are* at home – all the time!

It took me a few years before I was able to classify myself as a carer. I felt like a mother – because that is what I am – so to demand recognition for my caring role seemed wrong. It took me a long time to apply for the Carer's Allowance. I irrationally felt that others would probably need it more than me and, besides, the forms to apply for it were complicated. I didn't have the time or the energy to sit down and fill them in. When I did apply for this benefit it took me a long time to feel right about receiving it. It made me feel like I was no longer caring for my children for love, not if I was being paid for being a carer – which of course is ridiculous!

My caring role has been life changing for me, and the changes are not all positive. The first thing to change, or to go, was any prospect of a career after I had my children. Most mothers of disabled children do not work due to the huge difficulties associated with juggling bringing up a disabled child and working. This goes completely against the trend for most mothers of non-disabled children who do work. Of course, fathers can easily be affected in much the same way. Parents who carry on working can find their career options curtailed due to the effects that caring for a disabled child can have on their working lives. Having a disabled child puts added pressure on parents reducing their ability to sustain the efforts needed to advance professionally in their working lives. Statistics also show that it can be three times more costly to bring up a disabled child than a non-disabled child. However families are affected by their caring duties, there is usually a financial impact.

The next thing to disappear was my social life. It was just too difficult to find someone to babysit such demanding children when they were both not really able to tell anyone else what they needed, and wouldn't cooperate with a babysitter. How do you trust anyone else to be able to understand when your speech-disabled child is asking for a drink? How can you expect anyone else to know that your autistic child won't stay in his room because he is upset when the bedtime routine is not followed 'properly'? It is a lot to ask of anyone so we just did not ask, and got into the habit of rarely going out together. We do occasionally go out with other friends separately so that we do at least get a break, if not together – but you can't call it a shared social life. It is easy to see why the proportion of parents with disabled children who divorce is very high.

As for holidays, it is not so bad now but for about ten years it was so stressful going on holiday with my children that I really could not face it. I would pack up and go, uncomplainingly because my husband desperately needed it, and I did not feel able to put a dampener on things. But I could not enjoy it. There would be no sleep because of the strange environment. Cupboard doors would be opened and shut repeatedly. Light bulbs would be unscrewed, curtains pulled down and anything that could be moved was moved. There would be the social issues that would arise on the playground and if Peter fell out with anyone, then that would be it; he would not be able to move on from it for the whole holiday. After a holiday, I still felt like I needed a holiday!

These are all sacrifices that I was willing to make. Many other parents in the same position make these sacrifices too, but no carer should be expected to do these things without any help. So how do we access help?

Parents of disabled children can access some benefit payments that can make a difference to families in this position.

STATE BENEFITS FOR FAMILIES WITH A DISABLED CHILD

The government provides some state benefits that parents of disabled children can claim. It's not very much money but it is better than nothing, and if you find yourself giving up a job or career to be a carer these payments will help cushion the blow of losing a salary. These benefits are assessed and allocated based on the needs of the child.

Disability Living Allowance

This is a tax free non-means tested benefit for adults or children who have physical or mental disabilities (including mental health problems), and who need help with getting around. DLA is split into two parts:

- *Care component* – This is paid at the lower, middle or higher rate and is for people who need help with personal care.

- *Mobility component* – This is paid at the lower or higher level.

The amounts paid vary according to the level of disability and difficulty with mobility. Further advice on claiming for this can be obtained from the Direct Gov website, or the Department of Work and Pensions. Contact details are in my Useful Organisations and Web Resources section. It is important that you get the right help to fill out the form. While it is written in plain English it is long and can appear complex. First timers (or even some second or third timers!) will benefit from help to fill it in. I note that disability support groups like Contact A Family or the National Autistic Society also have information about it on their websites and advice and support can be accessed by contacting their helplines.

Carer's Allowance

This is a benefit that carers can apply for. You generally have to be looking after someone for at least 35 hours a week who gets Disability Living Allowance at the middle or higher rate care component. You have to be aged 16 or over and not studying for more than 21 hours a week. You can work if you receive Carer's Allowance but currently are not allowed to earn more than £95.00 per week (after deductions). Further information is available from the Direct Gov website or the Department of Work and Pensions.

Child Tax Credits

Families can claim for Child Tax Credits. If you have a child for whom you receive Disability Living Allowance at the higher rate for personal care the Child Tax Credit (CTC) you can claim can include an extra Disabled Child Element. Further information is available from the Direct Gov website or the Department of Work and Pensions. However unlike the other benefits tax credits are means tested. There are lots of well-known examples where the Inland Revenue have overpaid one year and then taken back the next. We found it difficult to interact with them and many families who have relied on tax credit income can find it taken away with no discussion. Yes it did happen to us.

Blue Badge Scheme

The Blue Badge Scheme issues parking permits for disabled people. With this permit they may park in special disabled bays on streets and in car parks. If your child receives the higher rate of the mobility component of Disability Living Allowance or is registered blind then they qualify automatically for a blue badge. If your child has a permanent and substantial disability which means they cannot walk, or which makes walking very difficult, they may after assessment qualify for a blue badge from your council. Under certain circumstances you may qualify for a blue badge for a child under two years old. Check eligibility criteria with your local council and also on the Direct Gov website.

Flexible working arrangements

About four years ago I saw a newspaper advert placed by the Department of Trade and Industry about the right for parents with disabled children under 18 to ask their employers for flexible working arrangements. I pointed this out to my husband who sceptically agreed to investigate this at work. To our amazement we found that his employer was happy for him to fit his working hours into four days, leaving time free to help with our children's therapies. Having a parent present who was listening to the therapist and could take notes on how to apply the therapy at home has made a huge difference to our children's outcomes. It also enabled my husband and me to spend some time together without the children when they were at school – it gave us a break.

From April 2009 parents who have a disabled child aged 18 or under and parents of non-disabled children aged 16 and under have the right to ask their employer for flexible working hours. The employer must take the request seriously and is obliged to find ways of enabling flexible working arrangements to work. Parents must not be penalised for trying to exercise their right to flexible working and if their request is refused they have a right to appeal to a tribunal. Further details are available on the Direct Gov website.

PARENTAL LEAVE AND TIME OFF IN EMERGENCIES

Parents are usually entitled to take a maximum of four weeks parental leave in a year. This is usually to be taken in weekly blocks but parents of a disabled child can take it by the day or at the rate of a few days at a time to fit in with their caring duties. Parental leave is usually unpaid but check with your employer to clarify this point. Employees also have the right to take a reasonable amount of time off work to deal with an emergency involving a dependent.

SOCIAL SERVICES AND CARER'S ASSESSMENTS

It has recently been estimated that 80 per cent of parents who care for a disabled child would describe themselves as at breaking point. As a carer you have the right to have a carer's assessment through social services to establish what *your needs* are as a carer, as well as any needs your child may have. Although the right to have an assessment exists, provision seems to be patchy with some carers I know being offered access to assessments via the professionals involved in their child's care, while others with comparable caring duties are not offered one. I was not offered one, so assumed for a long time that I must not need one! It was because of the old 'there are plenty of people worse off' argument. I suppose this may also have been because up until recently, children with an IQ of over 70 were not eligible for the services of the Children's Disability Team, which was of course discriminatory. They used to give services to physically disabled people with IQs of over 70 so they have now changed their remit. Whether you are offered one or not, as the parent of a disabled child aged 18 or under, or adult offspring aged 18 or over (our children grow up!) then you are entitled to one. Although social services can assess your child's needs too, it is also vital to focus on your own needs as a carer. It can pave the way to your receiving assistance such as:

- help with housework
- short breaks so that you can spend some time on your own or with your partner
- emotional support
- changes to equipment or adaptations to the home
- advice about benefits you may claim
- advice about combining working with caring or advice about returning to work
- help to access further education or training for yourself
- health advice to ensure your own needs are being met.

Your social worker will then develop a care plan based on the services you are entitled as needing to help you in your caring role, and will also complete an assessment of your child's needs. The support and services you have been assessed as needing should be outlined in the plan along with information about how they will be provided to you. Your support can be provided by social services or you may be offered Direct Payments which enable you to have more control over the help you need in your caring role. The Direct Gov website gives more details about carer's assessments and Direct Payments. We took the plunge and requested a carer's assessment. I did so with some trepidation, not being someone used to having anything to do with social services. Be aware that it is relatively easy to get a carer's assessment but if you want any actual help to come out of this process you will have to be very clear about what you need and stick to your guns. Carers often have to fight to get the needs of the people they care for met, but our needs are important too and we should also fight for ourselves to have the help we need.

A FEW OTHER THOUGHTS
Disabled children have historically had less access to leisure and social activities than their non-disabled peers. They are also more likely to be excluded from school and are more likely to live in poverty. Giving disabled children improved access to social and leisure activities can improve their outcomes. The government has put millions of pounds into a funding package to change completely the way disabled children's services are delivered to families. One of the provisions under this programme is that young people who are on the higher rate of Disability Living Allowance may have access to funding either through social services or £1000.00 per year in Direct Payments. This money may be spent on services aimed at giving that young person some independence, and the parents and other family members a break. You can find out more by downloading the following government document: *Aiming High for Disabled Children: Better Support for Families 2007* (DCSF 2007). The spending of the money is audited and there are restrictions on how it may be used.

There are also carers' support groups – some of them are listed in my Useful Organisations and Web Resources section. These provide information seminars, leaflets, support on claiming benefits and emotional support. I have even heard of the carers' group for my area organising pampering days for carers. Apart from offering the opportunity for a short break they enable carers to meet others with similar caring responsibilities.

Checklist

* If you are in a caring role, accept it and look after yourself accordingly, meeting your own needs as well as those of the person you care for.

* Contact your children's disability team and ask for a carer's assessment. Your GP or health visitor can make the referral if you don't feel able to do so yourself. You don't even have to know what you want, just say you are trying to find out about what might help you in your caring role. They often have access to information or sources of funding that we can't access.

* Try to access a good babysitting service or respite care provider through your health visitor, social worker (if you have one), or similar health/social care professional.

* If you choose the care provider well, you will be able to relax knowing your child is cared for and will benefit from your break and be better able to care for your child as a result.

* Join a carers' support organisation.

* Find out about, and get help with applying for, any state benefits you may be entitled to.

* If you work find out about flexible working arrangements.

* Join a parent support group relating to your child's condition.

* If your child has mobility problems, or you have difficulties with getting around that are associated with any medical condition or special needs that they may have, contact your local council to see if they qualify for a blue badge (a disabled parking badge).

* Encourage your child to take any opportunity to join in fun activities either through school or otherwise. If our children are occupied and happy, it helps us. We worry less and we can focus on the important things in life.

Chapter 8

THE DISABILITY DISCRIMINATION ACT

How is it Relevant to Your Child at School?

Provision for pupils with special educational needs is underpinned by the *Education Act 1996* and is obtained through schools making their own provision for pupils using their special educational needs budgets or through the statutory assessment process. Some pupils with special educational needs may also have disabilities. It does not follow that this will include all pupils with special educational needs. Similarly, not all pupils who have disabilities will have SEN.

Just as the rights of children with special educational needs are protected by law, the rights of disabled pupils in our schools are also similarly protected. The *Disability Discrimination Act 1995* deals with unlawful discrimination that might happen in everyday life because of a person's disability. To begin with it did not cover education, but was amended by the *Disability Discrimination Act 2001* that came into effect in 2002. This amendment created a duty for schools to not discriminate against children on the basis of their disability. I will discuss in this chapter the legislation as it applies to England and Wales. Those living in Northern Ireland and Scotland will be covered by separate laws, although in the case of Scotland there is some overlap.

According to the terms of the *Disability Discrimination Act 2001*, 'subject to the provisions of Schedule 1, a person has a disability for the purposes of this Act if he has a physical or mental impairment which has a substantial and long-term adverse effect on his ability to carry out normal day-to-day activities'.

The Act says that it is not lawful for schools to discriminate against pupils for a reason related to their disability in delivering things like:

- admissions
- exclusions
- education and associated services, including:
    - delivering the curriculum
    - teaching and learning
    - sporting events
    - music and drama opportunities
    - school trips
    - the serving of school meals.

THE DUTIES OF SCHOOLS

There is a duty under the Disability Equality Duty (Part 5A of the *Disability Discrimination Act 1995*, inserted by the *Disability Discrimination Act 2005*) for schools to take steps not to treat disabled pupils 'less favourably' and to make reasonable adjustments to make certain that disabled pupils will not be at a 'substantial disadvantage' at school compared to their non-disabled peers. They have to comply with the Disability Equality Duty to write, publish and implement a Disability Equality Scheme and promote disability equality. You can find out more about the Disability Equality Duty and access the statutory codes of practice for England, Wales and Scotland at www.dotheduty.org and the Equalities and Human Rights Commission website. The EHRC supercedes the old Disability Rights Commision, which set up the 'do the duty' website.

In terms of state schools, the LEA or governing body is likely to be ultimately responsible for ensuring disability equality. If your child's school is not run by the LEA find out which body is responsible for it. Most schools should have been ready to take on the new responsibilities of the Disability Equality Duty by December 2006 by writing and implementing a Disability Equality Scheme. All schools should have had their Disability Equality Scheme in place by December 2007. These policies can be accessed by parents and are usually available through the school website. The Disability Equality Scheme should outline all the ways in which the school is planning to promote equality of opportunity and eliminate discrimination both in accessing the curriculum and in participating in the wider life of the school. The duty applies in England, Wales and Scotland although there are different arrangements for Scotland owing to differences in Scottish legislation. The *Disability Discrimination Act 1995 Part 4: Code of Practice for Schools,* the *Disability Discrimination Act 2001* and the *Disability Discrimination Act 2005* can all be accessed through the Equality and Human Rights Commission website or the Office for Public Services Information website respectively.

The *Duty to Promote Disability Equality: Statutory Code of Practice, England and Wales* (DRC 2005) says that in terms of school, achieving equality of opportunity may in fact involve treating disabled people 'more favourably' than their non-disabled peers. True equality of opportunity cannot be achieved simply by treating all people exactly the same.

The organisation responsible for the school, or the 'responsible body' must ensure that the school does not discriminate against a disabled child in terms of its admissions policy, its delivery of education and related services or by excluding a pupil because of a reason relating to his disability. These things may happen because of a disabled pupil being treated, without any justification, less favourably because of their disability. It may also happen because the school fails to take steps to make reasonable adjustments to ensure that pupils are not placed at a substantial disadvantage.

WHAT DOES IT MEAN TO TREAT A PUPIL LESS FAVOURABLY AND WHAT DOES IT MEAN TO BE AT A SUBSTANTIAL DISADVANTAGE? WHAT ARE REASONABLE ADJUSTMENTS?

Schools must not treat disabled pupils less favourably and they must make reasonable adjustments to ensure disabled pupils are not at a substantial disadvantage compared to other pupils in the school. The following examples illustrate this:

- A child who has dysgraphia (handwriting difficulties) has been given a laptop under the terms of his statement for the purposes of recording his schoolwork. He is prevented from using it in class even though it is available and the child knows how to use it effectively to produce work. The teacher is not confident in using IT and tells the child to hand write his work like everyone else. He is unable to finish the work in the time allowed due to his slow handwriting, even though he knows how to carry out the task. The teacher has failed to facilitate the use of the laptop by the child with no justification. Therefore the child has been treated less favourably and has been at a substantial disadvantage compared to other pupils because of his disability. A *reasonable adjustment* would be if the child was permitted to use the laptop to record work because he was incapable of writing and this is an effective way for him to record his work.

- Another example of a pupil being treated *less favourably* may be where a hearing impaired child who lip reads struggles to hear the teacher in class. The teacher continually turns away from the class to write on the board and the pupil can't read his lips properly. He misses a lot of the lesson and is unable to carry out the associated writing task to the level he is capable of. Therefore the child has been treated less favourably and has been at a substantial disadvantage compared to other pupils because of his disability. A *reasonable adjustment* would be where the teacher ensures that he remains facing the class so that the pupil can lip read.

- Another example of treating a pupil less favourably could be where a pupil with visual impairment cannot access written materials in class because they are not in an accessible format. As a result the child cannot access the curriculum like their peers. Therefore the child has been treated less favourably and has been at a substantial disadvantage compared to other pupils because of their disability. A *reasonable adjustment* would be if the school arranged for this pupil to have an appropriate assessment to find out how the child could best access written course materials.

Sometimes it is necessary to appear to treat a pupil more favourably than other pupils so that reasonable adjustments can be made, and to prevent them from being treated less favourably.

- A pupil who has an autistic spectrum disorder is grouped in a low/average ability set for maths. This is an appropriate set for him to be in but there are a number of children in the class who have behaviour problems and are frequently noisy and rowdy.

The noise bothers this pupil and he is unable to concentrate. Due to the stress of the noise levels he cannot effectively access the curriculum. Therefore the child has been treated less favourably and has been at a substantial disadvantage compared to other pupils because of his disability. The Head of Maths decides to make *reasonable adjustment* and takes into account the boy's response to the noise levels and the impact on his learning. He places him in the higher group where behaviour is better and the class is quieter. The higher group is following a more advanced curriculum than the boy was previously following. To meet the boy's learning needs the Head of Maths modifies the boy's curriculum by giving him differentiated work to carry out in his new class. On the face of it the boy is treated more favourably as he is placed in a better working environment, even though he is below the level of attainment of the new class, but the school knows that the Disability Equality Duty provides for this. The boy is able to access the curriculum in his new group.

WHAT IF MY CHILD HAS BEEN DISCRIMINATED AGAINST? WHAT ARE MY OPTIONS?

If parents feel that their child is placed at a substantial disadvantage because he is treated less favourably and the school has failed to make reasonable adjustment, what can be done about this?

- In the first instance we can discuss matters with the school.

- If parents are not satisfied they can then consult the governing body of the school.

- If discussions do not go well there are mediation services that we can access through the LEA and also, the Equality and Human Rights Commission offers a casework and conciliation service that you might be able to access.

- Other sources of help are through our county councillors, MPs and other representatives.

However, legislation exists, with quite clear guidelines about what constitutes disability discrimination and schools should be well aware of their obligations. If you have tried to discuss the matter with the school or have used mediation services to no avail you may consider appealing. The following section looks at how appeals may be made.

WHERE CAN I APPEAL?

- For appeals about school admissions you must appeal to the admissions appeal panels (please seek contact details from your LEA).

- For appeals about school exclusions you must appeal to the exclusion appeals panels (please seek contact details from your LEA).

- You may be able to take a claim of disability discrimination to the First-tier Tribunal (Special Educational Needs and Disability). You must make your claim to them within six months of the discrimination occurring and they will then inform you as to whether or not you have a case. If you win your claim the First-tier Tribunal (Special Educational Needs and Disability) can tell the school to put in place disability training for staff or it can tell the schools to change their policies or procedures.

CONCLUDING NOTE

Schools must expect that at some stage disabled pupils will attend the school, and should have policies and strategies in place that provide for resourced and specific provision to be made *before* the arrival of any particular disabled pupil in school. It is not enough to wait until a disabled pupil joins the school, and then to hurriedly make provision by making changes that just apply to the one pupil. Robust policies must exist that could make it possible for any disabled pupil to access the curriculum and take part in the life of the school. This is because it may already be too late in the term to allocate any necessary funding to meet a child's needs thereby placing him at a substantial disadvantage. For what it is worth, I have the distinct impression from my dealings with schools that although the new legislation might have come in, the financial back-up that schools need to enable them to not discriminate is just not there. Certainly in my own children's school, good as it is, there appears to have been a somewhat slow awakening to the duties imposed by the disability discrimination legislation and teachers who really should know 'all the answers', very evidently do not. This is why it is essential for parents to have some understanding of their children's rights under the *Disability Discrimination Act* as summarised above. As with the *Education Act 1996*, if you don't ensure your children's rights are safeguarded, nobody else is going to do it for you.

Checklist

* It may not necessarily follow that a child with special educational needs has a disability.

* Establish whether your child has a disability under the terms of the *Disability Discrimination Act*. You can check this by looking at Schedule 1 of the *Disability Discrimination Act 2001*.

* If you think your child has been treated unfairly due to their disability consider *how* they may have been treated unfairly – has the school treated your child less favourably without justification or failed to make reasonable adjustment?

* Talk to your child's teacher and exhaust any procedures to discuss matters with the head teacher or governing body if appropriate.

* Ask for copies of the school's disability equality strategy and their disability equality policy. Does it make adequate provision for the school to make reasonable adjustments to prevent pupils from being at a substantial disadvantage? Does it prevent pupils with disabilities from being treated less favourably?

* Consider whether the school has failed to take steps to make reasonable adjustments to ensure that disabled pupils are not placed at a substantial disadvantage in comparison with non-disabled pupils, without justification.

* At the same time get advice from one of the parent support bodies, government organisations or voluntary organisations.

* If you wish to consider a complaint, take specialist advice from the appropriate organisations.

CONCLUSION

In Britain we have health and education services that are free at the point of access. We have legislation to ensure that children with special educational needs have their needs met and a law that stops schools and LEAs from discriminating against disabled children. So why doesn't it always work?

It all comes down to money and effort. Put simply, if you don't fight for your child's needs, nobody else is going to do it for you. This book has provided a framework for parenting a disabled child pro-actively to access the resources you need that has worked for us and it can easily work for you and your children as well.

It is unlikely that knowing your stuff and assessing your child's needs will make you popular with your local NHS Trust, local education authority or your children's school. However, it is also true to say that your children are unlikely to 'grow out of their disability' or have their needs met if you just wait and see what happens. It is our experience that there is a plethora of excuses which these authorities hide behind. It is up to you to hold them to account. It has worked for us.

This book is a tool kit of tactics and advice that has helped us to succeed in improving the quality of our children's lives. It contains all the information we wish we had known at the start of our fight to have our children's special educational needs met at school. Sadly we have had to find out most of this information the hard way. This has cost us dearly in lost opportunities, heartache and anguish, lots of tears, and for Peter five wasted, unhappy years at primary school.

You have all the information we have now assembled over the years at your fingertips. Use it. Nobody else will do it for you if you don't.

Remember the Guerrilla Mum Mantra: Don't take no for an answer, never give up. If in doubt, telephone, email and write letters.

USEFUL ORGANISATIONS AND WEB RESOURCES

Parents are often very much in the dark when faced with finding out about the resources that exist to help children with disabilities or special educational needs. Professionals sometimes assume that we already know what is out there to help, or simply don't think to discuss this with us. Helpful organisations are listed below.*

I. GOVERNMENT ORGANISATIONS

Department for Children, Schools and Families
Sanctuary Buildings
Great Smith Street
London
SW1P 3BT
Tel: 0870 000 2288
Email: info@dcsf.gsi.gov.uk
Website: www:dcsf.gov.uk
Contact the DCSF for information about the law and resources in England and Wales.

Department for Children, Schools and Families Publications Department
PO Box 5050
Sherwood Park
Annesley
Nottingham
NG15 0DJ
Tel: 0845 602 2260
Email: dcsf@prolog.uk.com
Website: www.dcsf.gov.uk
The *Special Educational Needs Code of Practice* is relevant to both England and Wales and can be downloaded through the DCSF website or by post free of charge from this department.

Department for Education
The Department for Education was formed on 12 May 2010 and is now responsible for education and children's services. All statutory guidance and legislation linked to from this site continues to reflect the current legal position unless indicated otherwise, but may not reflect Government policy. Please see the website for contact details.
Website: www.education.gov.uk

*Most of the organisations in this section will be useful to those in Scotland and Northern Ireland too, but for specific information on the law and policy in those countries see the dedicated sections at the end.

Equality and Human Rights Commission
Arndale House
The Arndale Centre
Manchester
M4 3AQ
Helpline: 0845 604 6610
Email: info@equalityhumanrights.com
Website: www.equalityhumanrights.com

Ofsted
Royal Exchange Buildings
St Ann's Square
Manchester
M2 7LA
Tel: 08456 404 045
Email: enquiries@ofsted.gov.uk
Website: www.ofsted.gov.uk

Office of Public Sector Information (OPSI)
102 Petty France
London
SW1H 9AJ
Email: Via enquiry form on website
Website: www.opsi.gov.uk

Patient Advice and Liaison Service (PALS Online)
Website: www.pals.nhs.uk
Contact your local PALS office by:
• phoning your local hospital, clinic, GP surgery or health centre and ask for details of the PALS
• phoning NHS Direct on 0845 46 47
• searching the office directory on the PALS Online website (link above).

Teachernet
Department for Children, Schools and Families
Sanctuary Buildings
Great Smith Street
London
SW1P 3BT
Tel: 0870 000 2288
Textphone/Minicom: 18001 0870 000 2288
Email: Via contact form on website

Tribunals Service Special Educational Needs and Disability
2nd Floor Old Hall
Mowden Hall
Staindrop Road
Darlington
DL3 9BG
Tel: 0870 241 2555 (SEN and discrimination helplines)
Email: sendistqueries@tribunals.gsi.gov.uk
Website: www.sendist.gov.uk
Contact the Tribunals Service for special educational needs appeals and disability discrimination appeals.

II. SUPPORT FOR PARENTS AND CARERS

Carers UK
20 Great Dover Street
London
SE1 4LX
Tel: 020 7378 4999
Email: info@carersuk.org
Website: www.carersuk.org/Home

Contact A Family
209–211 City Road
London
EC1V 1JN
Helpline: 0808 808 3555
Email: helpline@cafamily.org.uk
Website: www.cafamily.org.uk

Local Government Ombudsman
PO Box 4771
Coventry
CV4 0EH
LGO Advice Line: 0300 061 0614
Email: Via online enquiry form
Website: www.lgo.org.uk

National Parent Partnership Network
8 Wakeley Street
London
EC1V 7QE
Tel: 0207 843 6058
Email: nppn@ncb.org.uk
Website: www.parentparnership.org.uk

III. EDUCATION, CHILD PSYCHOLOGY AND CHILDREN'S RIGHTS

Advisory Centre for Education (ACE)
1c Aberdeen Studios
22 Highbury Grove
London
N5 2DQ
Tel: 0808 800 5793
Email: ACE prefer to receive enquiries about education via their telephone helpline
Website: www.ace-ed.org.uk

British Psychological Society
The British Psychological Society
St Andrews House
48 Princess Road East
Leicester
LE1 7DR
Email: enquiries@bps.org.uk
Website: www.bps.org.uk

The Children's Legal Centre
University of Essex
Colchester
CO4 3SO
Tel: 01206 877 910

Child Law Advice Helpline: 08088 020 008
Email: clc@essex.ac.uk
Website: www.childrenslegalcentre.com

General Teaching Council for England
Whittington House
19–30 Alfred Place
London
WC1E 7EA
Tel: 0370 001 0308
Email: info@gtce.org.uk
Website: www.gtce.org.uk

Independent Panel for Special Educational Advice (IPSEA)
6 Carlow Mews
Woodbridge
Suffolk
IP12 1EA
Tel: 0800 018 0423 (helpline)
0845 602 9579 (tribunal advice)
Email: IPSEA prefer enquiries to be made through their telephone helpline
Website: www.ipsea.org.uk

IV. BULLYING

Bullying UK
702 Windsor House
Cornwall Road
Harrogate
HG1 2PW
Email: help@bullying.co.uk
Website: www.bullying.co.uk

Kidscape
2 Grosvenor Gardens
London
SW1W 0DH
Helpline: 08451 205 204
Email: Kidscape prefer to receive queries through their telephone helpline
Website: www.kidscape.org.uk

V. HOME EDUCATION

Education Otherwise
PO Box 325
King's Lynn
PE34 3XW
Helpline: 0845 478 6345
Email: Via enquiry form on website
Website: www.education-otherwise.org

Home Education Advisory Service
PO Box 98
Welwyn Garden City
Hertfordshire
AL8 6AN
Tel: 0170 737 1854
Email: enquiries@heas.org.uk
Website: www.heas.org.uk

VI. SPECIFIC DISABILITY SUPPORT GROUPS

Afasic (Unlocking speech and language)
1st Floor
20 Bowling Green Lane
London
EC1R 0BD
Tel: 0845 355 5577 (helpline)
Email: By online query form on website
Website: www.afasic.org.uk

The British Dyslexia Association
Unit 8
Bracknell Beeches
Old Bracknell Lane
Bracknell
RG12 7BW
Tel: 0845 251 9002
Email: helpline@bdadyslexia.org.uk
Website: www.bdadyslexia.org.uk

Climb (Children Living with Inherited Metabolic Diseases)
Climb Building
176 Nantwich road
Crewe
CW2 6BG
Tel: 0800 652 3181
0845 241 2172
Email: info.svcs@climb.org.uk
Website: www.climb.org.uk

Downs Syndrome Association
Langdon Down Centre
2a Langdon Park
Teddington
TW11 9PS
Tel: 0845 230 0372
Email: info@downs-syndrome.org.uk
Website: www.downs-syndrome.org.uk

Dyspraxia Foundation
8 West Alley
Hitchin
Herts
SG5 1EG
Tel: 04162 454 986 (helpline 10am – 1pm)
Email: dyspraxia@dyspraxiafoundation.org.uk
Website: www.dyspraxiafoundation.org.uk

Mencap
123 Golden Lane
London
EC1Y 0RT
Tel: 020 7454 0454
Email: information@mencap.org.uk
Website: www.mencap.org.uk

National Autistic Society
393 City Road
London
EC1V 1NG
Helpline: 0845 070 4004
Email: nas@nas.org.uk
Website: www.nas.org.uk

Resources for Autism
858 Finchley Road
Temple Fortune
London
NW11 6AB
Tel: 020 9459 3222
Email: admin@resourcesforautism.
org.uk
Website: www.resourcesforautism.
org.uk

STEPS
Warrington Lane
Lymm
Cheshire
WA13 0SA
Tel: 01935 750271
Email: info@steps-charity.org.uk
Website: www.steps-charity.org.uk
This is a charity that supports people
with a lower limb difficulty or
walking difficulties.

VII. USEFUL WEBSITES

Department of Work and Pensions
www.dwp.gov.uk

Direct Gov
www.direct.gov.uk
Access this website for a range of
information about things such as
blue badges, social services, direct
payments, caring for someone,
occupational therapy, mental health
and lots of other subjects.

Do the Duty
www.dotheduty.org

Every Disabled Child Matters
www.ncb.org.uk/edcm/home.aspx

**ICAN (information about speech and
communication disorders)**
www.ican.org.uk/TalkingPoint

VIII. WALES

**Equality & Human Rights
Commission in Wales**
3rd Floor
3 Callaghan Square
Cardiff
CF10 5BT
Helpline Wales: 0845 604 8810
Email: wales@equalityhumanrights.com
Website: www.equalityhumanrights.
com/wales

**Special Educational Needs Tribunal
for Wales**
Unit 32
Ddole Road
Enterprise Park
Llandrindod Wells
Powys
LD1 6PF
Helpline: 015797 829 800
Email: tribunalenquiries@wales.gsi.
gov.uk
Website: http://wales.gov.uk/
sentwsub

Welsh Assembly Government
National Assembly for Wales
Cathays Park
Cardiff
CF10 3NQ
Tel: 0300 060 3300 or 0845 010
3300 (English)
0300 060 4400 or 0845 010 4400
(Welsh)
Email: webmaster@wales.gsi.gov.uk
Website: http://wales.gov.uk
Contact the Welsh Assembly for
information about the law and
resources specific to Wales.

IX. NORTHERN IRELAND

For information about the law and resources in Northern Ireland contact:

Department of Education
Rathgael House
Balloo Road
Bangor
BT19 7PR
Tel: 028 9127 9279
Email: mail@deni.gov.uk
Website: www.deni.gov.uk

NI Human Rights Commission
Temple Court
Belfast
Northern Ireland
BT1 1NA
Tel: +44 (0) 28 9024 3987
Tel: +44 (0) 28 90247844
Email: Via website enquiry form
Website: www.nihrc.org

SENDO Special Educational Needs and Disability (Northern Ireland) Order 2005
www.deni.gov.uk/index.htm

NI Direct Government Services
www.nidirect.gov.uk

X. SCOTLAND

Contact the Scottish Executive for information about the law and resources in Scotland.

Enquire (The Scottish Advice Service for Additional Support for Learning)
Children in Scotland
5 Shandwick Place
Edinburgh
EH2 4RG
Tel: 0131 222 2425
Email: info@enquire.org.uk
Website: www.enquire.org.uk

Equality and Human Rights Commission in Scotland
The Optima Building
58 Robertson Street
Glasgow
G2 8DU
Helpline: 0845 604 5510
Email: scotland@equalityhumanrights.com
Website: www.equalityhumanrights.com/scotland

The Scottish Executive
Victoria Quay
Edinburgh
EH6 3QQ
Tel 0131 244 7066
Email: ceu@scotland.gsi.gov.uk
Website: www.scotland.gov.uk

Special Needs and Information Point (SNIP)
14 Rillbank Terrace
Edinburgh
CH9 1LL
Tel: 0131 536 0583
Email: snip@btinternet.com
Website: www.snipinfo.org

UPDATE (Scotland's National Disability Information Service)
Hays Community Business Centre
4 Hays Avenue
Edinburgh
EH16 4AQ
Tel: 0131 669 1600
Email: info@update.org.uk
Website: www.update.org.uk

REFERENCES

Department for Children, Schools and Families (2001a) *Special Educational Needs (SEN): Code of Practice.* Available at www.teachernet.gov.uk/_doc/3724/SENCodeofPractice. pdf, accessed 7 May 2010. Crown Copyright.

Department for Children, Schools and Families (2001b) *Special Educational Needs (SEN): A Guide for Parents and Carers.* Available at www.teachernet.gov.uk/_doc/3755/4163_ A5_SEN_GUIDE_WEB[4].pdf, accessed 7 May 2010. Crown Copyright.

Department for Children, Schools and Families (2002) *The SEN Toolkit.* Available at www. teachernet.gov.uk/wholeschool/sen/teacherlearningassistant/toolkit, accessed 7 May 2010. Crown Copyright.

Department for Children, Schools and Families (2007) *Aiming High for Disabled Children: Better Support for Families 2007.* Available at www.dcsf.gov.uk/everychildmatters/ healthandwellbeing/ahdc/AHDC, accessed 7 May 2010. Crown Copyright.

Department for Children, Schools and Families (2008) *Bullying Involving Children with Special Educational Needs and Disabilities – Safe to Learn: Embedding Anti-Bullying Work in Schools.* Crown Copyright.

Department for Children, Schools and Families, Teachernet (2010) *Teachernet Sample Anti-Bullying Policy.* Available at www.teachernet.gov.uk/management/atoz/a/ antibullyingpolicy, accessed 16 June 2010. Crown Copyright.

Department for Education and Skills (2004) *Removing Barriers to Achievement: The Government's Strategy for SEN.* London: Department for Education and Skills. Crown Copyright.

Disability Rights Commission (2002) *The Code of Practice for Schools: The Disability Discrimination Act 1995.* London: HMSO. Crown Copyright.

Disability Rights Commission (2005) *The Duty to Promote Disability Equality: Statutory Code of Practice for England and Wales.* Available at www.dotheduty.org/files/Code_of_ practice_england_and_wales.pdf, accessed 16 June 2010. Crown Copyright.

Disability Rights Commission (2006) *The Duty to Promote Disability Equality: Statutory Code of Practice, Scotland.* London: HMSO. Crown Copyright.

Lamb, B. (2009) *Lamb Inquiry: Special Educational Needs and Parental Confidence.* Available at www.dcsf.gov.uk/lambinquiry, accessed on 16 June 2010. London: Crown Copyright.

Tribunals Service Special Educational Needs and Disability (2010) *How to Appeal an SEN Decision: A Guide for Parents.* Available at www.sendist.gov.uk/Documents/ FormsGuidance/ForParents/How_Appeal_SEN_Decision_April10.pdf, accessed 16 June 2010. Crown Copyright.

ACTS

Disability Discrimination Act 2001. London: HMSO.

Disability Discrimination Act 2005. London: HMSO.

Education Act 1996. London: HMSO.

The Education (Special Educational Needs) (England) (Consolidation) Regulations 2001. London: HMSO.

School Standards and Framework Act 1998. London: HMSO.

INDEX